WANCHAI

ARTHUR HACKER'S
WANCHAI

(previous pages) *A distant view of Wanchai showing right Praya East, left Kellett Island.*

An Odyssey Publication © 1997
Text © Arthur Hacker 1997

Published by The Guidebook Company Limited, Hong Kong

All rights reserved. No part of this book may be translated, reproduced or transmitted in any form, or by any means, electronic, mechanical, photocopying or otherwise, without the prior permission of the publisher.

Photo & illustrations credits:

Most of the illustrations in this book are a part of the Arthur Hacker Collection of old photographs, prints and postcards of Hong Kong, Macau, China and Japan. The reproduction rights of this collection are managed by the Stock House Photoagency, 23/F 88 Lockhart Road, Wanchai, Hong Kong. Tel: 2866 0887 Fax: 2866 2212.

Grateful acknowledgment is made to the following:

I would like to thank all those kind people who helped me gather the material for this book: Larry Allen, Ken Barrett, Phillip Bruce, Penny Byrne, Nick Demuth, Saul Lockhart, Nancy Lau, Alan Macdonald, Peter Mann, the Hong Kong Government, Sarah Monks of The Hong Kong Trade Development Council, David Perkins, Dr E. G. Pryor, Spring Water Wong and David Smith, phillumenist extraordinary, whose former matchbox collection graces the pages of this book. My special thanks to the Hong Kong Tatler, the South China Morning Post and What's On, where some of this material has already been published in a somewhat different form, and Airphoto International, Magnus Bartlett, Cameraman, Rosanne Zimmerman and Terry Duckham-Asia Pix.

Books by Arthur Hacker:

Hacker's Hong Kong (with David Perkins)
Historic Postcards of Hong Kong
Hong Kong in Posters
The Hong Kong Visitors Book

Co-ordinating Editor: Jane Finden-Crofts
Designer: Teresa Ho Kit Mei
Cover Design, Art Direction: Harvey Symons, Margaret Ng
Maps: Tom Le Bas, Louis Papachristou

Odyssey Publications / The Guidebook Company Limited, Hong Kong
G/F 2 Lower Kai Yuen Lane, North Point, Hong Kong.
Tel: (852) 2856 3896 Fax: (852) 2565 8624.
E-mail: odyssey@asiaonline.net

ISBN: 962-217-465-5

Printed in Hong Kong

Wanchai from the air.

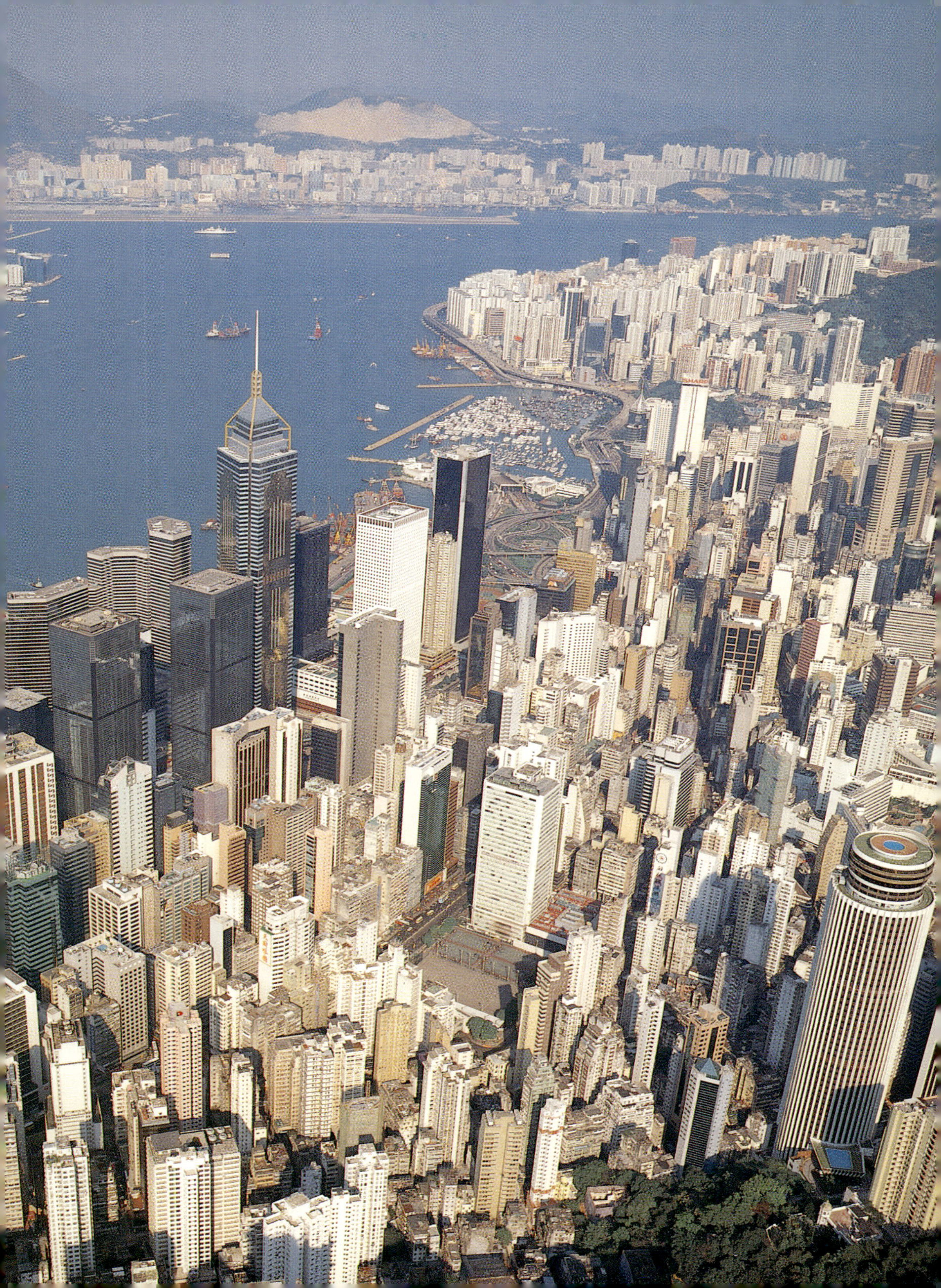

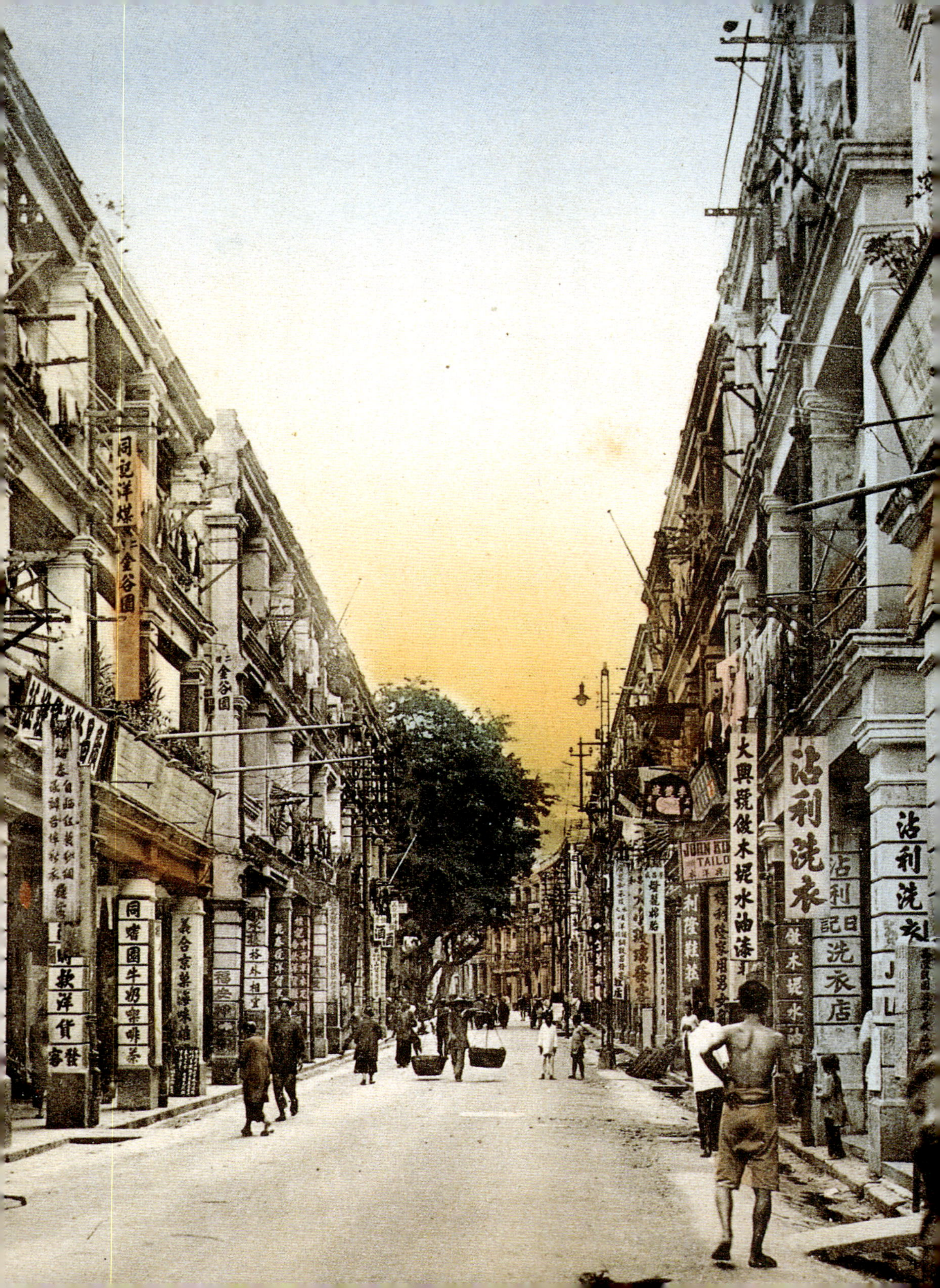
同記洋煤
金谷園
大興號欽木泥水油漆
沾利洗衣
沾利洗衣
沾利記日洗衣店

CONTENTS

Introduction
8

The Early Years
9

Distressful Bread
33

The Years Between
58

The World of Suzie Wong
86

Modern Wanchai
111

Wanchai 2010
138

Queen's Road East at the turn of the century.

INTRODUCTION

Wanchai means 'little bay' in Chinese. It is a rather unromantic and basic name for what was nothing more than a beach on an obscure, poverty-stricken island, somewhere off the remote southern shores of the vast Manchu Empire. However, as Macau and Canton became more wealthy, Hong Kong began to emerge from total obscurity. The early story of Hong Kong is inextricably linked with the history of those two cities.

There are many ways of looking at history. Mere facts, taken out of context, are easily misinterpreted. What seems to have been inevitable is that, sometime during the last century, there would have been a clash between the Manchu Empire and the Empires of the West, if only because of the arrogant nature of these two diametrically opposed civilizations.

There is little point, one hundred and fifty years later, in blaming either China or Britain for the wars that were fought between them. It is even more ridiculous to blame a modern Briton or Chinese. Imperialism has been an unpopular political philosophy in Britain for half a century and China today is no longer run by a foreign dynasty of Manchu Emperors.

Modern Wanchai is an exciting place. Like Holland, most of it is built on land reclaimed from the sea; from a small bay a great, glitzy metropolis has emerged, which is Wanchai today. What, if anything, was there before 1841 is uncertain.

THE EARLY YEARS

PREHISTORY

Archaeologists reckon that in the Ice Age Hong Kong lay inland, about thirty miles from the coast. However, so far no early human remains from this period have been discovered. There are no missing links. No Peking Man. No Piltdown Man—not even a fake one.

There are a few prehistoric sites in the Territory, dating back to the Stone Age. Some fine examples of Neolithic pottery have been unearthed, as well as Stone and Bronze Age weapons and tools: axes, adzes, daggers and fish-hooks have been found. These have been dug up in the remoter parts of the Territory. There are also some interesting rock carvings. Most of these are close to the sea. They are linear in design, with mainly geometric or spiral patterns. There is a particularly beautiful zoomorphic carving at Big Wave Bay, which is a mere six metres above sea level at high tide. This was discovered as late as 1970 by a Scotsman serving in the Royal Hong Kong Police. If any similar carvings ever existed in heavily populated areas like Wanchai, it is almost inevitable that they were destroyed years ago.

Little is known of the people who made these carvings. They called themselves the Yao people. Han historians describe them as being barbaric, tattooed, short-haired and expert at fighting on the water. So what has changed? Two thousand years later creatures of this kind can still be seen cruising around Wanchai late at night. They are called sailors.

THE HAN INVASION

Very little has been written about the Yao people. Legend has it that there was a certain Emperor who was having trouble with a rival chieftain. The Emperor swore an oath that he would give his youngest daughter's hand in marriage to anyone who would cut off this enemy's head and bring it to him. One day, to his horror, his pet dog turned up with the rebel chief's head and dropped it at his master's feet. The strong-willed Princess insisted that the Emperor keep his vow; the Princess and the dog were married. They had six offspring. The Yao tribe, who were descended from this unorthodox union, seem to have been rather proud of their ancestors. It is reported that they refused to wear Chinese clothes, but instead dressed up to look like dogs, sporting canine head-dresses and even tails. There is a theory that the Tanka, or boat people, are their descendants. This theory is probably a bit of Han Dynasty propaganda and is not very popular with the fisherfolk of Aberdeen.

Hong Kong was first colonized, not by the British, but by the Chinese in 220BC, when the Imperial Army of the Emperor of Tsin defeated the Yao people and Hong Kong became an obscure part of the Chinese Empire. Four years later, the Tsin Dynasty fell and the region became an independent kingdom under a Chinese monarch. The Han armies conquered it a century later.

Tuen Mun in the New Territories was quite an important port during the Tang Dynasty (618-907), when the first foreign ships from India and Persia began to arrive in the region. After the fall of the Tang Dynasty, the region became an independent kingdom once again, until it was reconquered by the Sung armies in the tenth century.

THE SUNG PRINCESS

The Mongols, those wild horsemen from the North, attacked China in 1127 and captured most of the Sung Emperor Kao Tsung's family; but his ten year old daughter escaped and fled South. Fortunately, her party ran into a band of Royalist militia commanded by a member of the powerful Tang clan, who owned Hong Kong Island at the time. Tang hid her in Kam Tin, in the New Territories, where she married his son Tang Tzu-ming. After a truce had been signed between the Emperor of China and the Mongols, officers were sent all over the Empire to look for the Princess. This worried the Tang family, because the marriage had taken place without the consent of the Emperor.

However, the young Princess returned boldly to the Imperial court, taking along her unwilling husband. The Emperor magnanimously forgave the Tangs. The Princess did not like court life and soon returned to rural Kam Tin, where, we are told. she lived happily ever after.

THE END OF THE SUNG DYNASTY

A century and a half later, the Mongol hordes of Kublai Khan descended on China and delivered the final death blow to the tottering Sung Dynasty. The Emperor's two younger brothers escaped. The eldest, Yi Wong, a child of nine, was proclaimed Emperor by the loyal Chinese. The boy Emperor and his followers fled South, pursued relentlessly by ferocious Mongol horsemen. Eventually they found refuge at Silvermine Bay (Mui Wo) on Lantau, which is Hong Kong's largest outlying island. Poor Yi Wong died on Lantau and his younger brother, Wei Wong, aged seven, succeeded him. He was the last Sung Emperor. In 1279, Wei Wong and his entourage were trapped between a Mongol army and a Mongol fleet and is thought to have drowned while attempting to escape. So it was that China came to be ruled by a foreign conqueror, the Great Khan—Kublai Khan—the founder of the Yuan Dynasty; and consequently Hong Kong became a colony of the Mongols.

THE PIRATES AND THE PORTUGUESE

Piracy has always been the plague of the South China Coast. For centuries the 'Sea Dwarfs', as the Japanese buccaneers were known, plundered and robbed the coastal provinces. The Portuguese helped the Chinese fight them off and, as a reward, they were allowed to establish a 'Dwarf Catching Station' at the mouth of the Pearl River. This Portuguese enclave is now called Macau.

The first great Chinese pirate was known as Nicholas Iquan by the Portuguese. This former Macau merchant had once been an interpreter with the Dutch East India Company before becoming a sea rover. In the last years of the Ming Dynasty,

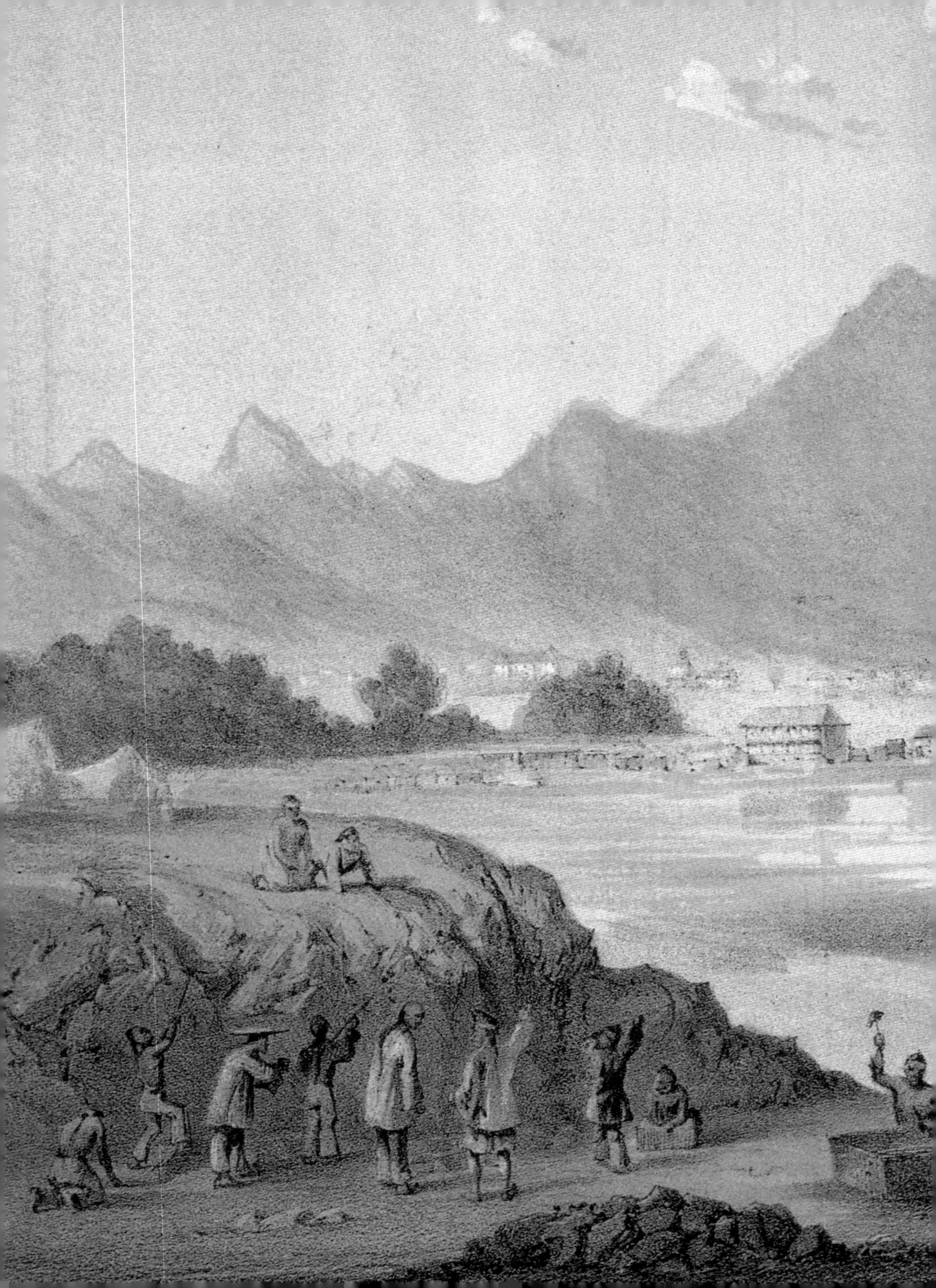

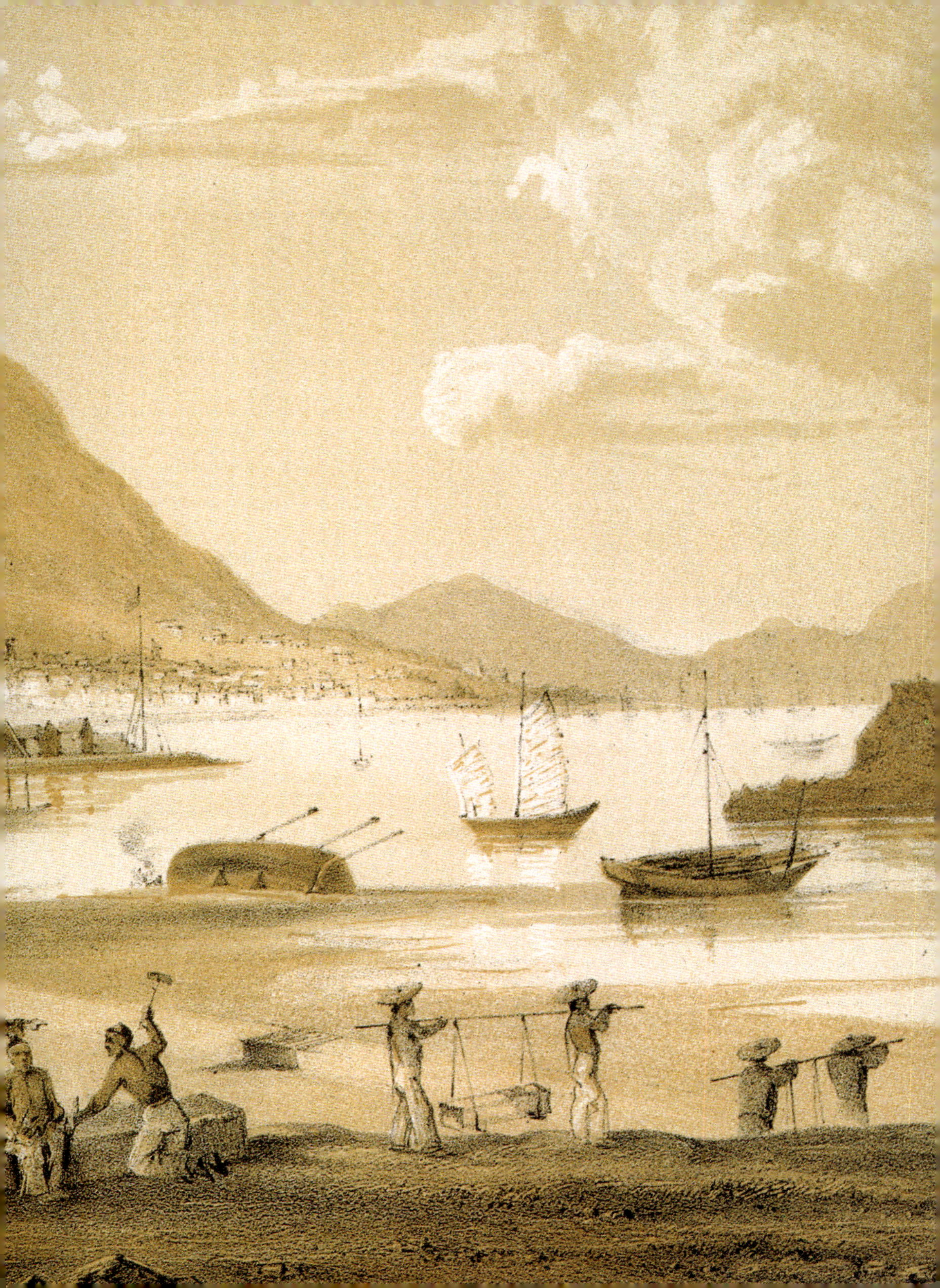

(previous pages) Hong Kong from Causeway Bay. Kellett Island can be seen on the right of the picture. A lithograph by W. Heine and Eliphalet Brown Jr, c. 1853.

he had over 1,000 pirate junks under his command and was raiding the whole length of the China coast, wreaking havoc and destruction.

The Ming Emperor had no effective navy. The only way he could control Iquan was by offering him, in 1628, the post of Commander of the Imperial fleet. Admiral Iquan's job was to suppress piracy in the South China Sea. This he did brilliantly until the Manchu invasion in 1644.

When the Chinese Mings were obviously losing, Iquan decided to change sides. During the negotiations he was kidnapped by the treacherous Manchus and his followers were slaughtered. He was later executed.

Iquan had a son by a Japanese woman. In the West he is generally known as Koxinga. Unlike his treacherous father, he was loyal to the Ming cause. In 1659, Koxinga descended on Nanking with a massive fleet. The city lay at his mercy. Unfortunately he delayed the final assault in order to celebrate his birthday. It was a great party and everybody got drunk. It was then that the Manchus attacked. Koxinga was forced to retire to Taiwan with what remained of his battered fleet.

Koxinga returned to buccaneering. He was so successful that the Manchus had to adopt a 'scorched earth' policy. They ordered everyone living on the coast to move seventeen miles inland upon pain of death. For a few years nobody lived on Hong Kong Island at all. After the edict was lifted, most of the original population never returned. Instead, the Tang Punti villages were taken over by itinerant Hakkas, who were a tribe of wandering and homeless Northerners. Hakka means 'Guest people' in Chinese.

The 'scorched earth' policy had been a disaster. The farmers and fisherman, having been forced to abandon their homes, turned to piracy in order to survive. A century and a half later their descendants still roved Hong Kong waters. One of the most successful was Mrs. Cheng, the widow of a pirate chief. In 1810, she defeated a combined force of ninety-three Manchu war junks and six Portuguese vessels at Chek Lap Kok, off Lantau island, the site of the new airport.

At the height of her power, Mrs. Cheng commanded two hundred and seventy ships and 30,000 buccaneers. She operated *(following pages) The foreign factories at Canton before their destruction in 1856.*

out of a number of robber nests, including one at Quarry Bay, a couple of miles east of Wanchai.

Mrs. Cheng was notoriously promiscuous. Her sex life was her undoing. One of her lieutenants, Kuo Po-tai, who had once enjoyed her favours, changed sides in a fit of pique and became a Manchu admiral. Not to be outdone, her reigning favourite, Cheung Po-tsai, also joined the Tartar oppressors. He too was made an admiral and persuaded Mrs. Cheng to surrender. Deserted and betrayed by her lovers, poor Mrs. Cheng had no other choice. Unfortunately, the Manchu emperors did not employ women admirals.

CANTON AND THE EAST INDIA COMPANY

It is not surprising that the Chinese regarded all foreigners as pirates—most of them behaved like them. The Portuguese adventurer Simao d'Andrāde arrived in his caravels in 1519. Without permission from the Chinese, he built an illegal fort at Tuen Mun. From this 'trading post' his ships plundered and terrorized the Pearl River Delta. Chinese retribution was swift. The great military Mandarin, Wang Hung, destroyed the fort and sunk most of d'Andrāde's ships. It was thirty years before trade was resumed.

After the Portuguese had been allowed to settle in Macau, other European nations attempted to trade with China. On the whole, they did not create a very good impression. The Dutch, on the assumption that whoever controlled Macau controlled the China trade, attacked the 'City of the Name of God' in 1622. They were butchered by a tiny makeshift citizen army, made up mainly of tradesmen, sailors, servants, pensioners, Jesuits and ferocious African slaves.

In 1637, the English sea captain John Weddell attempted trade directly with China. When the Chinese refused to do business with him except through Macau, he arrogantly sailed his fleet of four ships up the Pearl River. The Chinese thought he was a pirate and sent down fire-boats to meet him. Weddell's reaction was violent. He embarked on an orgy of destruction: pillaging villages, sinking junks and murdering innocent Chinese villagers.

The Early Years   15

The City QUAN

FU, or CANTON from Nieuhof

Plate 44

Fifty years later, trade restrictions were eased with the West and, in 1685, Canton was opened up to foreign ships. China was, at that time, self-sufficient and the West had very little to offer in exchange for tea, silk and porcelain—apart from silver. This metal was the basic currency of China and at the time was plentiful in the West. Trade was only allowed to be conducted through those great national monopolies, the East India Companies: the English, Dutch, French and Swedish, who traded directly with a Chinese monopoly called the Co Hong merchants.

The multinationals of today seem rather insignificant when compared with these monumental organizations. At one time the Dutch East India Company had a standing army of 17,000 soldiers. They employed 20,000 men and owned over two hundred ships. The English John Company's armies conquered most of India. In spite of this, both companies had very few employees in Canton, where they were confined to a tiny ghetto. The only way they could keep commerce going was by fawning to the Chinese mandarins and paying them enormous bribes. This was how business was done in Canton. They didn't like it, but they accepted it because everybody was making such a gigantic profit. If a little grovelling and squeeze kept the mandarins happy—so what!—provided it oiled the wheels of commerce. This period is often called the 'Golden Age of China Trade'. I can't think why. But it was all very cosy until everything went wrong.

There were many causes for the disastrous era that followed. The Napoleonic War had completely disrupted world trade. The Spanish Empire in South America had collapsed and in the chaos of revolution and civil war which followed, silver mining in Peru and Bolivia was disrupted. The British reduced the duty on tea. As an extraordinary amount of the tea bought in Canton by the Europeans was smuggled into England from the Continent, the European companies suffered enormous losses. The French and Dutch East India Companies had grown too big and went bankrupt. The Swedish Company sensibly just stopped doing business. It was no longer profitable.

Europe had changed. The spirit of liberty and equality dominated politics. The massive, autocratic, semi-independent monopolies controlling trade and making their own wars were no longer tolerable in the age of reason. Even before 1834, when the John Company lost its monopoly, a new breed of animal had descended on Canton. These were the first of the Taipans—the interlopers. Hard, ruthless men like Doctor William Jardine, James Matheson and James Innes, the unspeakable Laird of Dunkinty.

There was not enough silver in the West to pay for the tea. The simplest way of getting silver was by selling the Chinese opium. As it was illegal to import opium into China, the interlopers resorted to smuggling. The self-righteous John Company claimed that it obeyed the laws of China because its ships carried no opium. This may have been true, but it is also true that the Bengal opium the British sold in China was bought in India from the Company. The other great smuggling nation was America, who purchased its opium in Turkey.

The interlopers were proud, independent Scottish and English merchants. Their sea captains and sailors were often Napoleonic War veterans. Britain was the greatest maritime power the world had ever known. It is therefore not surprising that the attitude of the interlopers was one of chauvinistic, righteous anger. Their belligerent argument was: why should the victors of Trafalgar, who had defeated Napoleon, have to grovel to and bribe a bunch of corrupt, heathen Manchu officials in order to warm the teapots of England. Canton was the only port where they were allowed to trade. William Jardine's single-minded purpose was to destroy the old system and open up other ports in China to trade. He was a very determined man, known to the Chinese as the 'Iron-Headed Old Rat'. When it comes to devising nicknames, the Chinese are invariably brilliant.

TEA, SILVER AND OPIUM

There are two questions that historians have never been able to answer satisfactorily. They are: *why* did the British drink so much tea? And *why* did the Chinese consume so much opium? Tea was drunk in every country in Europe, where it was often much cheaper than in England, but it was only consumed in small quantities. The craze for tea drinking did not seriously

An opium den. Thomas Allom, c. 1843.

The Early Years 21

affect the economy of any country except Great Britain and her colonies. Conversely, opium was easily available and legal almost everywhere in the world; but only China, where it was illegal, was devastated by this horrible drug. Surprisingly, China has never had an alcohol problem.

Opium is a very emotive subject. Consequently it is easy to over-simplify the causes of the Opium Wars and judge them by late 20th century moral values. The anti-British lobby predictably blames the British for poisoning the Chinese people with opium. The anti-China lobby point out that the corrupt Manchu mandarins made this possible. They were up to their necks in the trade to the extent where the Governor of Kwangtung and Kwansi Teng Ting-chen's opium suppression force was actually hired by the opium smugglers to carry their opium up river to Whampoa. Opium had been grown in China for centuries, but the quality was poor and the supply was never sufficient to meet demand.

There are also anti-French lobbies and anti-American lobbies. There is even, I am told, a small anti-Irish faction who put the blame squarely but unfairly on the massive bovine shoulders of Bernardo O'Higgins, whose revolutionary activities in Chile and Peru put up the price of silver. Perhaps it is best to describe the whole business diplomatically as an 'accident of history' and leave it at that.

Silver was certainly one of the key issues. The Chinese economy was built on a silver standard. For three hundred years there had been a steady flow of silver from the West. In normal times, the price of an ounce of silver was around a thousand copper cash. When the flow was reversed by the enormous outflow of silver to pay for opium, the price of silver began to fluctuate erratically. This played havoc with the Chinese economy. At one stage it reached a high of 1,600 cash for an ounce of silver. There was even talk of going back to the ancient jade standard. Something had to be done about it.

Commissioner Lin was sent down to Canton by the Emperor to sort everything out. He behaved impeccably by Confucian standards. Captain Elliot, on the British side, was a patient and compassionate man, who was desperately keen to do the right thing as a Protestant Christian gentleman. They were both conscientious and capable public servants. They both loathed the opium trade. However they never met. Lin did not consider it proper for a high Manchu official to discuss mutual problems with a foreign barbarians whose only duty it was to obey. While Elliot was trying to arrange talks, Lin was writing letters, or rather instructions, to Queen Victoria as though she were a naughty child. It could never have occurred to him that she might not be amused by being addressed as an 'honourable barbarian chieftainess', nor would she be likely to 'tremblingly obey' any of his edicts. It is evident from Lin's diaries that he actually believed the popular Chinese fiction of the time, that the Son of Heaven ruled the world and every other country was a vassal state of China.

Both the diaries and letters of Commissioner Lin and Captain Elliot are fascinating reading when compared to each other. They were both civilized men, but from entirely different civilizations. It is tragically obvious that there was great black hole of misunderstanding between China and the West: a gigantic vacuum of ignorance, prejudice and age-old tradition that left absolutely no common ground. From both points of view it was like trying to conduct negotiations with creatures from outer space. A clash of some sort was inevitable. It would have happened sooner or later. Opium was the spark.

THE OPIUM WAR

Nowadays, an old Chinese sailing junk can occasionally be seen beating her way through Victoria harbour like a dying moth. It sometimes takes one of these clumsy vessels three days to make the passage. Imagine such a craft, armed only with old muzzle-loading cannon, trying to out-manoeuvre and out-fight a lethiferous little iron steamer like the *Nemesis* equipped with 32-pounder guns. Imagine the effect a single broadside from a 74-gun man-of-war like HMS *Blenheim* would have on one of these craft. The Chinese Imperial war junks had been pretty ineffective against Mrs. Cheng's pirate fleet. Against the firepower of the Royal Navy, they did not stand a chance.

Procrastination has always been a popular tactic of Chinese generals. The favorite maxim of Sun Tzu, the great Chinese strategist, was: 'To subdue the enemy without fighting is the acme of skill.' Neither the procrastinating military mandarins or Sun Tzu ever seem to have realized that this tactic is not very effective against an enemy that goes straight for the jugular. The British commander, Sir Hugh Gough, was notoriously aggressive. Attack was his only known military tactic. At the Battle of Sobraon, during the First Sikh War, when told that he was short of ammunition, he was heard to mutter, 'Thank God! Then I'll be at them with the bayonet.' In the Opium War there were no major land battles and very few casualties. It was a surprisingly bloodless campaign for a general like 'Paddy' Gough, who was famous for running up 'butcher's bills' whenever he fought a battle.

With complete mastery of the seas and an effective army, the British plan was simple. It was to sail up the Yangtsze, capture a few towns, blockade the Grand Canal and make demands direct to the Emperor. The objective was to secure a safe island base in China, open up a few other ports to trade and persuade the Manchus to recognize them as equals. The British were fed up with being called barbarians and being treated as though they were a subject race.

The Ching Emperor was in a weak position. The Manchus were a foreign dynasty, descended from the Tartars who had overrun China and evicted the Ming emperors. There were frequent Chinese rebellions and the Emperor's position was never very secure. The occupation of a small barren island by an outer barbarian and the opening up of another five ports to trade seemed a small sacrifice to pay to preserve the Dragon Throne, which was in constant danger of toppling.

The Manchus did not, at the time, seem to have regarded the ceding of Hong Kong

A Chinese cavalryman.

to the British as a real loss of sovereignty. They saw it more as establishing a new barbarian ghetto, like Macau, as a temporary trading post for a troublesome vassal. It was expected that when the British ran out of food and ammunition, the Manchus could take it back.

However, the demand that the barbarians should be treated as equals with the Chinese was another matter. The idea that Queen Victoria should have the same status as the Son of Heaven was ludicrous in Chinese eyes. However, because of the threat, it was politic to humour the barbarians for the time being.

In 1841 Hong Kong was ceded to the British. However, it was only after the Arrow War (1856-60) that the foreign legations were established in Peking and China began to open up to the West.

The almost total lack of any real understanding between the mandarins of China and Western diplomats has always been a problem for both civilizations. It still is.

A Chinese soldier.

EARLY WANCHAI

Commodore Sir J.J. Gordon Bremer, on Captain Elliot's instructions, raised the British flag at Possession Point on 26 January 1841, officially taking possession of the island of Hong Kong for Her Majesty Queen Victoria.

He was not at all pleased when he discovered that the day before, on 25 January 1841, Captain Sir Edward Belcher of HMS *Sulpher* had already raised the Union Jack, claimed the island for the Queen, drunk Her Majesty's health and given three hearty cheers. Later Belcher took some readings 'on a hillock, within a stone's throw of the houses of Morrison Hill' to establish the longitude and latitude of the island. He named the valley behind the hill after himself. This was the beginning of the Royal Navy's long association with Wanchai.

The character of early Wanchai was influenced enormously by the first Land Sale on 14 June 1841, when Captain William Morgan, on behalf of Jardine, Matheson & Co, bought a Marine Lot at East Point for £150. East Point was rather isolated. There was a sandy beach between Jardine's first godowns at

East Point and the company's two other marine plots at the foot of Morrison Hill.

A couple of years later, Lieutenant T.B. Collinson of the Royal Engineers drew a panoramic sketch of the area. It shows Jardines, the beach and the buildings of the Morrison Education Society on the top of the hill. Above it was Lover's Rock, where even today unmarried girls burn joss sticks and pray for a husband. On the harbour side of Morrison Hill there was a drop down to the rocky edge of the water; behind it Queen's Road East ran through the green rice paddies of Belcher Valley. This name was never popular for homonymous reasons and was soon changed. The story goes that an amorous mapmaker fell in love with a young lady and proposed to her at a picnic. When she rejected him, he named the picnic site Repulse Bay. A few weeks later he proposed to her again at Belcher Valley and was accepted. He renamed the place Happy Valley to commemorate this joyful occasion. Happy Valley is the home of the sport of kings and there has been racing here since 1846.

The Morrison Education Society was founded by J.R. Morrison, the son of Robert Morrison, who was the first Protestant Missionary in China. The elder Morrison translated the Bible into Chinese and compiled the first English-Chinese dictionary. His mission work was not so distinguished—only four converts in twenty-seven years of pious endeavour. J.R. Morrison, like his father was a brilliant linguist. He was Acting-Colonial Secretary when he died, at the age of twenty-nine, in 1843.

Moving west, next to Morrison Hill, was Hospital Hill. It was here that Parsee merchant Herjeebhoy Rustomjee planned to build his Seaman's Hospital. He offered to donate $12,000, but unfortunately went bankrupt just as the scheme got going and Jardine's had to pick up the bill. In 1873, Jardines sold the Seaman's Hospital to the Navy for $35,000 and a new hospital, called the Royal Naval Hospital, was built on the site.

To pay for the Seaman's Hospital, Admiral Charles Shadwell sold the Royal Navy Hospital Ship HMS *Melville* for $35,600, thus making a profit of $600. In recognition of this financial coup Hospital Hill was renamed Mount Shadwell. The Naval Hospital is long gone, but today there are still a number of modern hospitals and clinics clustered around the hill, including the Ruttonjee Hospital, named after Jehanghir Ruttonjee, another Parsee merchant, who contributed two million dollars towards the construction of the Ruttonjee Sanatorium which previously stood on the site.

Hong Kong's first Chief Justice, John Walter Hulme, also had a house on this hill. Chief Justice Hulme was one of the great characters of early Hong Kong. Hulme and the second Governor of Hong Kong, Sir John Davis, did not get along. This is not surprising, because Davis believed in the divine right of governors and Hulme stood for the independence of the courts.

The problem was that the two magistrates, Major William Caine, the founder of the Hong Kong Police, and Charles Hillier, had little legal training. Consequently, when the people they had convicted appealed to the Supreme Court, Hulme invariably let them off on a legal point. This infuriated the Governor, but there was little he could do about it.

In the end Davis resorted to a 'dirty tricks' campaign. He complained in a private letter to the British Foreign Secretary, Lord Palmerston, that Hulme was an habitual drunkard. Much to his surprise, the British Government demanded that these charges be proven.

Two years earlier, at a ball aboard HMS *Agincourt* given by Admiral Sir Thomas Cochrane for the Chinese Commissioner Keying, Hulme had made a bit of an exhibition of himself by dancing the hornpipe with Mandarin Tung, a corpulent Manchu Tartar who was married to an Imperial Princess. Edward Cree, who was there, described the scene:

'Tung fat, and enveloped in his silk coats, cap and peacock's feather and satin boots, with soles 2 inches thick, and capering like an elephant, and the Judge anything but grave, flinging his long skinny legs, encased in breeches and black silk stockings, in all directions, his long visage and protuberant nose, his bushy head and broad grin, having anything but a judge-like appearance.'

Hulme's defence was that 'his occasional unsteady gait was due to varicose veins'. The Executive Council found him guilty, but its verdict was overruled by the Secretary of State in London. Hulme was reinstated and the unpopular Governor resigned.

Spring Gardens by Murdoch Bruce, 1846. On the right is the Blenkin Rawson House, where Governor Sir George Bonham lived.

Just below Hospital Hill was the Wanchai Road. Up a small lane off the Wanchai Road, at the back of the Ruttonjee Hospital, is a flight of steps leading to a stone gateway, which has a cross carved on its granite arch. It is said that the Royal Navy gigs would land their sick here. In the 1840s it was on the waterfront. A little further on was a fashionable residential area called Spring Gardens. There is a story that it was named after a dubious London pleasure garden that had been closed by the puritanical Oliver Cromwell in the dreary days of the Commonwealth, because it was a 'rendezvous for ladies and their gallants', where, as John Evelyn the diarist wrote, they consumed 'forbidden fruits, trifling tarts, salacious meats and bad Rhennish'.

Hong Kong's Spring Gardens was far more respectable. Lindsay & Co constructed Hong Kong's first European building, the Albany Godown, near here. There were a number of pleasant houses on a promenade beside the sea. In fact, Spring Gardens is probably the name of the Blenkin Rawson house, which can be seen on the right in Murdoch Bruce's famous lithograph. Bruce was Hong Kong's Overseer of Roads. Apart from being a gifted amateur artist, he was a keen musician and a craftsman so skilled with the lathe that he made his own bagpipes.

Blenkin Rawson & Co was not a famous company. It only operated for two years in the colony. The third Governor of Hong Kong, Sir George Bonham, moved into the building while he was waiting for Government House to be built. Bonham was known as the 'Model Governor', possibly because he was the first Governor to balance the colony's budget. The only way he could do this was by not paying his own salary. He also subscribed to the theory that 'the study of Chinese warped the intellect and undermined the judgement'. This might have had something to do with the fact that the previous Governor, the unloved Sir John Davis, had been an eminent Chinese language scholar. Today if you walk down Spring Garden Lane, with its quaint little shops, fast food outlets and rubbish collection point, it is difficult to imagine that a hundred and fifty years ago this district was the most fashionable residential area in Hong Kong and even the Governor lived there.

A few yards away was Larkins Pier. It was named after Captain Larkins, who also bought a plot of land at the June 1841 sale. His company Innes, Fletcher & Co had originally been started by James Innes, the notorious interloper and opium smuggler and sworn enemy of Dr Jardine. Larkins died of the pox in Macau in 1843.

The next landmark was Burn's Pier. It was named after D.L. Burn of Burn, MacVicar & Co, which sold both opium and insurance. D.L. Burn was a Justice of the Peace. The complex consisted of two hundred yards of sea wall with a godown and house as well as the pier.

Wanchai was not only the haunt of opium smugglers. It was an important area for shipping and ships' chandlers. This is reflected in street names like Sam Pan Street, Schooner Street and Ship Street. Close to Ship Street were the first Protestant and Catholic civilian cemeteries at St Francis Yard. Star Street, Moon Street, Sun Street and St Francis Street now stand on the site. The cemeteries were only used from 1841 to 1845. In 1889, the remains of fifty-five people were moved to Happy Valley. For reasons of superstition, nobody was particularly keen on developing the site, until Sir Paul Chater, the great Armenian entrepreneur who could never resist a bargain, persuaded the Hong Kong Electric Company to buy the vacant plot. They built Hong Kong's first power station on the land. There is still a road called Electric Street in the area.

Hong Kong is famous for its shopping and Wanchai was the place where it all started. The Canton Bazaar stood approximately where the Supreme Court Building is today, next to the great modern shopping and hotel complex that includes Pacific Place and the Conrad, Marriott and Shangri-La hotels. Appropriately, this is where the first Chinese traders opened their shops for business after Hong Kong became a British colony. These merchants came from Canton.

At the west end of Wanchai was a military cantonment with the Arsenal and Wellington Barracks. Having a couple of thousand troops stationed in the vicinity had its problems. Except when on duty, the troops were not allowed to rove the city of Victoria. Consequently they took their recreation in Wanchai. There were a number of taverns, brothels and mission houses to cater for their various needs. There were the occasional flare ups. One particular affray in July 1844 between soldiers of the 98th Regiment and the European residents of a lane near the bazaar, is worth recording. For once the civilians got the upper hand and a number of soldiers were beaten up.

There was talk around the barracks of a revenge attack

on the civilians the next night. Wisely, the military authorities sent a patrol to the area to prevent further trouble. Unfortunately, the officer commanding the patrol, Lieutenant Macdonald, arrested a civilian called Robinson whom he suspected of being involved in the fracas the previous evening. He took him back to the barracks, where he was subsequently beaten up by the vengeful soldiers.

Robinson took Macdonald to court and Chief Justice Hulme fined him $50. Macdonald refused to pay on the grounds that the court ' was at variance with the Mutiny Act.' This resulted in William Caine, the Sheriff of the Supreme Court, issuing a warrant for Macdonald's arrest. Unfortunately there was a shortage of bailiffs at the time and the man Caine sent around to arrest Macdonald was a private soldier in the British army who was on loan to the Court. Macdonald recognized the soldier, even though he was in civilian clothes, and had him arrested for 'disrespectful conduct'.

'The high-feeling which renders it worse than death to a British officer to submit to an unprovoked insult' provoked Macdonald to send Captain Jeffery of the 98th regiment around to Major Caine with an insulting note challenging him to a duel. Duelling was illegal in Hong Kong at the time and Major-General D'Aguilar, the commander of British Forces, arrested Macdonald and Jeffery. Macdonald had a lucky escape. Major Caine was a legendary swordsman and a crack shot.

Overlooking Wanchai was Scandal Point. After Sunday Service at St John's Cathedral, the fashionable would stroll along the heights behind Flagstaff House to a shady nook of trees. Here 'the congregation would pause awhile, and the scandalmongers got busy'.

In the early years Wanchai was little more than a thin stretch of land, about a mile long, running from Jardine's at East Point, where the Excelsior Hotel is today, to the military cantonment that began at Arsenal Street. Considering that the European male population of the whole of Hong Kong Island, not counting military and naval personnel, was around three hundred, few of whom lived in Wanchai, it is surprising that Wanchai had any recorded history at all.

*The 18th Royal Irish in action during the Opium War.
Sketched on the spot by Captain Stoddard RN, redrawn by Thomas Allom.*

*The Chinese Imperial Commissioner Keying. Seated on the left is Major-General d'Aguilar
and on the right is the Governor Sir John Davis. Major William Caine
is second from the left.*

DISTRESSFUL BREAD

The West first became aware of Wanchai's existence in 1857, when the 'Great Bread Poisoning Case' made headline news. The sensible Sir George Bonham had been replaced as Governor of Hong Kong by Sir John Bowring, an elderly man in his sixties. The disastrous governorship of Bowring gave a certain credibility to Bonham's ridiculous theory that 'the study of Chinese warped the intellect'. Bowring was reputed to speak over thirty languages. The poet Thomas Hood wrote of him:

> 'All kinds of gab he knows, I wis,
> From Latin down to Scottish -
> As fluent as a parrot is
> But far more Polly-glottish.'

He even translated the Chinese novel *The Flowery Scroll* into English. He was a former Member of Parliament who had fallen on hard times and sought government employment in the colonies. Bowring was a radical thinker, a Benthamite, an anti-Corn Laws lobbyist and Secretary of the Peace Society. Unfortunately, like many intellectuals, his actions seem to have been totally governed by petty emotions, rather than by the cold, logical, impartial reasoning of a great mind.

Bowring arrived in Hong Kong at the beginning of the Crimean War. His first wild, impulsive action was to sail away with the British fleet and most of the garrison to Siberia to fight the Russians, leaving Hong Kong totally undefended. This vainglorious attempt to invade Tsarist Russia ended in humiliation. The Royal Navy's landing at Petropaulowsky was repulsed easily by the Tsarist armies.

Before coming to Hong Kong, Bowring had spent three frustrating years as British Consul at Canton. Unlike other treaty ports, the traders were still confined to a tiny European ghetto area known as the 'Factories'. The reason for this restriction, according to Yeh Ming-chen, the Viceroy of Kwangsi and

Kwangtung, was one of security. Yeh claimed that he could not guarantee the safety of the merchants. This was probably quite true. There was also an added problem. The Chinese version of the Treaty of Nanking was written in such a way that it could be interpreted differently from the English version—and was, by Yeh.

Although in theory the Manchus had agreed to treat foreigners as equals, in practice they found this a very difficult thing to do. They did not try very hard. The concept of the equally sovereign nations was totally alien to everything that they believed. The British Government seems to have been prepared to tolerate this misconception. The instructions to Bowring were simple. Armed force must *not* be used. The right of a few troublesome merchants to walk around Canton was not worth fighting for and if the Manchus seriously believed that they were superior to everybody else, so what? It was not an acceptable reason for starting a war—but Bowring thought otherwise.

THE ARROW INCIDENT

The Acting British Consul in Canton was a fiery young man called Harry Parkes. He appears frequently in modern Chinese films as the arch-villain of British colonialism. He was one of those dangerous people who are totally without fear. For all his blustering and rashness he somehow managed to survive some hair-raising adventures. It was always his companions who ended up dead. He was an energetic and devious bully. Like Bowring, he was also a keen student of the Chinese language.

On 8 October 1856, Yeh's Mandarins arrested the Chinese crew of a lorcha called the *Arrow* in Canton harbour. The ship was Chinese owned, but she was registered in Hong Kong. According to the Supplementary

The chop of the Esing bakery.

Treaty of the Bogue, if the Manchus wished to arrest a Chinese sailor serving on a British registered ship, they had to apply to the British Consul. The arrest therefore appeared to be illegal.

Parkes immediately demanded the release of the crew. Yeh offered to return nine out of the twelve men arrested. Parkes then referred the matter to Sir John Bowring who, as Plenipotentiary, was his superior. Bowring issued Yeh with an ultimatum. Yeh reluctantly returned the prisoners—and there the matter should have ended.

But Bowring demanded an apology which Yeh, predictably, refused to give. Instead of letting the matter drop, Bowring, in spite of his instructions from London to avoid armed conflict, sent the Royal Navy up the Pearl River, where they bombarded Canton. The Manchus counter-attacked by burning down the Factories. The British did not have enough troops to capture and hold Canton, while the Manchus did not have the firepower to invade Hong Kong. The result was an uncomfortable, if temporary, stalemate.

During the period of phoney war which followed, the Royal Navy blockaded the Pearl River. Yeh resorted to guerilla warfare and put a price on British heads. This started a new industry. The odd drunk was murdered on his way home from the pub, but most of the heads that ended up on the walls of Canton came from Happy Valley Cemetery. Hong Kong's entrepreneurs did a brisk trade in grave-robbing.

Yeh Ming-chen, the Viceroy of Kwangsi and Kwangtung.

Distressful Bread 35

When the news of Bowring and Parkes' action eventually arrived in London a couple of months later, there was a tremendous row. Their case was not helped when it was discovered that the *Arrow's* registration had run out and she was not entitled to British protection at all. There was a great debate in Parliament. The Tories, who had opposed the colonization of Hong Kong in the first place, temporarily allied themselves with the Peelites and brought down the Liberal government of Lord Palmerston.

In two years of governorship, Bowring had attempted to invade Russia, had started a war with China and toppled the Liberal Government—not a bad beginning for a former Secretary of the Peace Society and a Liberal Member of Parliament. But there was more to come...

POISONED DAWN

The Manchu terrorist campaign continued with unabated fury. The steamer *Thistle* was captured by Yeh's militia, who beheaded the eleven Europeans on board. There was a proliferation of unexplained fires. The streets became unsafe. Local residents seldom ventured abroad unarmed. Most households employed a Malay guard armed with a musket to protect them. It was a city under siege. British troops supported by French and American sailors patrolled the dangerous streets. A month later, at dawn on 15 January 1857, Yeh's guerillas attacked the soft underbellies of the Europeans with Borgian cunning. Two or three hundred of Hong Kong's foreign residents were struck down with arsenic poisoning.

The diabolical plot was based upon the theory that the Chinese did not eat bread. They only liked rice. Therefore, by lacing the bread supply with arsenic, Yeh's murderous agents hoped to wipe out the European population of Hong Kong, leaving their compatriots unscathed. The conspiracy hopelessly misfired. The terrorists forgot that the large Indian community of Hong Kong also ate this barbarian foodstuff. They were early risers and took their breakfast before the Europeans. Consequently they were hit first. By the time most of the sleepy Europeans had dragged themselves out of the comfort of their warm feather beds, there were a lot of sick Indians; the terrible secret was out. As the *Hongkong Register* explained: 'The cause of sickness being apparent, we escaped it by not eating bread.'

Unfortunately no one seems to have thought about warning the Governor until it was too late and the Bowring family suffered terribly. Sir John wrote: 'It left its effect for some days in racking headaches, pains to the limbs and bowels.' The poisoners had used far too much arsenic and 'the excess of quantity led to immediate alarm—application of emetics, and speedy ejection of the perilous stuff'. Lady Bowring never really recovered. She left Hong Kong and died in Taunton on 27 September 1857.

But who was the villain who executed this ghastly plot? The suspicion fell on Cheong Ahlum, the proprietor of the Esing Bakery in the heart of Wanchai, where the bread had been baked. Early that morning at 8 o'clock, he and his family had sneaked out of Hong Kong aboard the steamer *Shamrock*, bound for Macau. Naturally he was the principal suspect. The Hong Kong Government was slow to react. If it had not been for a private citizen, W.M. Robinet, he could have easily escaped. Robinet hired a steamer called the *Spark* and set off in hot pursuit. Robinet was a man of action. However, not all of his actions were quite so public spirited. He was later involved in a massive insurance fraud in Peru and ended up in gaol.

When he arrived in Macau he discovered that Ahlum had already been taken into custody. The passengers of the *Shamrock* had been stricken by the poisoned bread. The Captain, Mr Antonio, was very suspicious and had detained Ahlum aboard the *Shamrock*, even though the baker's children were among the poison victims. Robinet persuaded the Macau authorities to arrest Ahlum. Eventually the Hong Kong police arrived in the steamer *Queen* and took Ahlum and his family back to the Colony the next day.

TRIAL BY JURY

The European community of Hong Kong was badly shaken by the poisonings, even though there were no deaths. They

The Esing Bakery, where the poisoned bread was baked, stood in Queen's Road East near the Hung Shing Temple.

suddenly felt enormously vulnerable. Apart from the armed forces, there were only about five hundred of them, including women and children, isolated and exposed amongst a population of 70,000, often hostile, Chinese. The police had arrested everyone they could find who had any remote connection with the Esing Bakery. There were demands that Ahlum and his workers should be strung up outside the bakery, but Bowring stood firm. There would be no lynching. No summary executions. Ahlum appeared before the magistrate and was sent for trial before the Chief Justice: a sober, rather sickly Justice Hulme.

Appearing for the prosecution was the Attorney-General, Thomas Chisholm Anstey. He was a Tasmanian and former

Ahlum before the magistrate. He is the Chinese in profile. On his left is one of his wives. On his right is his father. From a drawing by M A Baptista, 1857.

Distressful Bread 39

Sir John Bowring, Governor of Hong Kong.

Member of Parliament for Youghal, in County Cork, who regarded it as his sacred duty to root out corruption in Hong Kong. He pursued this noble objective with the erratic fanaticism of a whirling dervish. Dr William Thomas Bridges and his creature Daniel Caldwell were his principal targets. They epitomized, in Anstey's eyes, all that was evil and corrupt in the Crown Colony. Fate decreed that Dr Bridges, who was also a lawyer, appeared for the defence.

The slanging match began with Anstey accusing Dr Bridges of 'violating professional etiquette' by visiting his clients in gaol without 'the intervention of an attorney'. Anstey won a technical point. It was his only victory.

Ahlum had been in his bakery in Wanchai at the time when the dough was mixed; but he had been taken there against his will by a reliable witness and had no opportunity to poison the bread. The only people who had not been arrested were two of Ahlum's foremen, who had escaped to China, and it soon became obvious that they were the guilty parties.

Ahlum had everything to lose by poisoning the bread. He owned the most successful bakery in Hong Kong. He had recently landed a highly profitable contract to supply the British military with vast quantities of biscuit. He had just bought the flour. The defence was that, having taken his children to Macau and on to China, he intended to return to Hong Kong to fulfil this lucrative contract. After all, hadn't he given his own children freshly baked bread and they also had become violently ill? It was just an awful coincidence that he had chosen that fateful morning to take his offspring to Macau. Everybody knows how the Chinese love children.

Anstey's case was that the machiavellian Ahlum had fed his children from a secret supply of unpoisoned bread and that the poor little things were only suffering from seasickness. It was a pretty feeble argument and failed to convince the jury. Determined to get a conviction, Anstey rashly appealed to the emotions of the jury—and blew his case. While admitting that there was not enough evidence to convict the defendants, he made the outrageous suggestion that it was 'better to hang the wrong men than confess that British sagacity and activity have failed to discover the real criminals'.

Mr Justice Hulme rebuked him sternly: 'I, in common with the Attorney-General, am desirous that justice should be done on the perpetrator of this crime, but hanging the wrong man will not further the ends of justice.'

On 5 February 1857, Cheong Ahlum was found not guilty by a majority of five to one. The Governor, the Chief Justice, the Attorney-General, Dr Bridges and the members of the jury had all eaten the poisoned bread.

Ahlum's acquittal was a triumph for British justice. What followed was not.

THE AFTERMATH

Bowring had Ahlum and the other prisoners rearrested as 'suspicious characters' under a hastily contrived ordinance 'for better securing the Peace of the Colony'. Most of the Chinese and British community thought that this was unfair. The leaders of the Chinese community suggested that, as a compromise, Ahlum and his companions should submit to 'voluntary banishment' from the Colony. Deportation ran against the grain because they had been found not guilty.

Bowring referred the matter to London. Meanwhile he composed a 'Hymn of Thanksgiving', which was sung at St John's Cathedral. At that time there was a shortage of civil servants in Hong Kong and, when the Colonial Secretary, Mr William Mercer, went on leave, Bowring appointed Dr Bridges to act in his place. As a special concession, Dr Bridges was allowed to carry on with his private law practice.

However, not everybody agreed that Ahlum should go unpunished. William Tarrant, the vitriolic editor of the *Friend of China* newspaper sued Ahlum for damages 'sustained in consequence of his having been poisoned by bread' and was awarded $1,010. Ahlum now owed a large number of people a lot of money. However, there was a proviso that, before he left the Colony, Ahlum must settle all his debts. When the Secretary of State instructed the Hong Kong Government to release Ahlum, his departure was arranged secretly and with great stealth by the venal Dr Bridges. In his new capacity of Acting Colonial Secretary, Bridges managed to spirit Ahlum out of the Colony one step ahead of his creditors, after having made absolutely certain that Ahlum had paid him his lawyer's fee first and probably a hefty bribe as well. Dr Bridges hit the jackpot, while nobody else received a penny.

Tarrant was furious! He attacked Dr Bridges' action in the *Friend of China*. Dr Bridges sued Tarrant for libel and was awarded £100 damages. This was the first shot in a war between the corrupt and the incorrupt that tore Hong Kong apart in the middle of the last century. If it had not been for this unseemly squabble, Wanchai would have been a very different place than it is today.

THE PRAYA SCHEME

It is easy to dismiss Sir John Bowring as an old fool. Nothing could be further from the truth. He was a visionary who possessed the misguided brilliance of a failed genius and the arrogance to match it. Unfortunately, he never understood that politics are about people and his tendency to treat others as his intellectual inferiors made him very unpopular.

In Bowring's time, the city was known as Victoria. It was virtually a one street town, the Queen's Road, which ran along the shore line between the Peak and the sea, with a few clusters of side streets in Wanchai, Western, Central, Happy Valley and East Point. What is now Des Voeux Road Central and Queen's Road East, was the waterfront. Like all great concepts, Bowring's Great Praya Scheme was simple. It was to build a sea wall from East Point to Navy Bay (Sai Ying Pun) and reclaim

Bowrington Canal at the turn of the century.

Sampans in the harbour.

Distressful Bread 43

a vast area of building land in the process. He decided to call the sea wall Bowring Praya. Hong Kong's first new town was planned in Wanchai, which he announced modestly would be called Bowrington (Bowring Town) after himself. This unfortunate choice of name did not add to his popularity.

The Praya Scheme was approved in principle by the Secretary of State for the Colonies, Henry Labouchère, and Bowring was instructed to start the massive reclamation work as soon as the funds were available. For years Bowring had squirreled away the money for his pet project, so all that was necessary was to persuade the Legislative Council to pass a bill and he could go ahead. There was opposition to the bill from an unofficial member, John Dent, but as the official members of the council were all civil servants and constituted an invincible majority, Bowring did not expect any problems. The first reading of the bill was predictably opposed by Dent, whose waterfront property would be affected by the scheme, but he was the only person who voted against it.

If everything had gone according to plan, Wanchai would be known today as Bowrington.

ELI BOGGS

In Hong Kong nothing ever goes according to plan. It was the arrest of the American pirate Eli Boggs that set in motion a chain of events which wrecked Bowring's grand design and almost destroyed his administration. On 4 July 1857, Eli Boggs, an American citizen, appeared before Hong Kong's Supreme Court charged with murder and piracy. Found innocent on the first count but guilty on the second, he escaped with an extraordinarily light sentence. Fact and fiction have become confused over the years and a lot of the saga of Eli Boggs is pure legend.

It is a fact that he did actually appear in court on those charges and conducted his own defence. In a speech of great power that lasted two hours, he claimed that he had been framed by Ma Chow Wong, a bumboat proprietor and wet fish merchant, and Daniel Caldwell, who at one time or another held the posts of Registrar-General, Assistant Superintendent of Police and Protector of the Chinese. Boggs virulently protested his innocence and accused them of being in league with pirates themselves.

George Wingrove Cooke, *The Times* correspondent, was in court that day. Describing Boggs, he wrote: 'His name would do for a villain of the Blackbeard class, but in form and feature, he was like a hero of a sentimental novel; as he stood the dock, bravely battling for his life, it seemed impossible that that handsome boy could be the pirate whose name had been for three years connected with the boldest and bloodiest acts of piracy. It was a face of feminine beauty. Not a down upon the upper lip; large lustrous eyes; a mouth with the smile of which might woo coy maidens; affluent black hair, not carelessly parted; hands so small and so delicately white as they would create a sensation in Belgravia; such was the Hongkong pirate Eli Boggs.'

Witness after witness told how 'E-loi', as the Chinese called him, had raided their ships. He generally took only silver and opium, which were easy to dispose of, leaving the rest of the cargo untouched. However, on one occasion he stole a box of sweets from the cabin of Mr Carvalho, the second officer of a Portuguese lorcha. The prosecution

Eli Boggs, the notorious American pirate.

Distressful Bread 45

was unable to find a witness who had actually seen him kill anyone. Nor was there any evidence that he was the captain of the formidable pirate fleet that launched the attacks.

Boggs was acquitted of murder, but the jury found him guilty of piracy. Instead of receiving the death penalty, he was sentenced to be transported for life, which was virtually nothing more than a slap on the wrist and a one-way ticket to the United States of America at the expense of the Hong Kong Government. It was a bewilderingly mild sentence. One can only speculate that Chief Justice Hulme, whose sentencing was generally considered rather severe but scrupulously fair, thought that there was some truth in Boggs' story. Both the Attorney-General Thomas Chisholm Anstey and Charles May, the Superintendent of Police, suspected that something highly irregular was going on.

The arrest of Boggs is generally credited to one-eared Bully

Street barbers in the Wanchai Road in the 1890s.

46 Wanchai

In 1898 there were 645 rickshaws on Hong Kong Island. Twenty years later there were over 2,000.

Hayes—a notorious American pirate, swindler and rogue who once made a living touring New Zealand as a 'nigger minstrel'. Apart from kidnapping South Pacific islanders and selling them off as indentured labour in Australia—a vile practice known as 'blackbirding'—his speciality was acquiring ships without paying for them. He also had a habit of abducting dusky South Sea maidens and generally had one or two aboard his ship.

If his story is to be believed, Boggs jumped overboard and swam for shore as two Royal Navy cutters closed in on his junk, which then blew up. Hayes, who was on board one the cutters, hurled himself into the water in hot pursuit. A strong swimmer, he soon caught up with Boggs and there was a flash of deadly steel as Boggs slashed at Hayes with his dagger. Hayes knocked the pirate out with a devastating right swing. Not

Distressful Bread 47

content with the £1,000 reward for Boggs's capture, Hayes made off with two of Boggs' silver-filled treasure chests.

It is a colourful story. But Bully Hayes seems to have been in Australia at that time, preparing to commit bigamy for the second or third time with a young lady called Amelia Littleton.

Eli Boggs was actually arrested in Bonham Strand, outside Ma Chow Wong's house, by Constable Barker on the orders of Mr Grand Pré, Caldwell's corrupt subordinate. There was rumour that Boggs was married to the daughter of one of Ma Chow Wong's concubines and that Ma Chow Wong used the girl to lure Boggs into a trap. Another story says that Boggs was visiting Ma Chow Wong to collect instructions for a pirate raid when he was arrested.

Boggs claimed at his trial that he had come ashore to shoot some birds for his crew, who were short of food. Although he was a bit of a dandy when it came to clothes, he was in rags at the time of his arrest. Something did not make sense.

After thoroughly re-questioning Boggs in Victoria Gaol, Charles May raided Ma Chow Wong's house. The police found hordes of goods pirated from ships. They also found papers that proved conclusively that Ma Chow Wong was a pirate and a receiver of stolen property. Caldwell's Chinese name, 'Sam-kwei', appeared frequently in 'the shop-books of pirate Wong'. This damning evidence proved that Caldwell was on his payroll.

Ma Chow Wong was tried and convicted, in spite of Caldwell's outrageous attempt to save him. He had acted as Caldwell's informer for years and they appear to have run a protection racket together. Their victims were the pirate chiefs of the Pearl River Delta. If the buccaneers refused to pay 'squeeze', Ma Chow Wong informed Caldwell and Caldwell either arrested them or tipped off the Royal Navy, who annihilated them.

Caldwell thus gained an awesome reputation as a pirate catcher and was popular with the Royal Navy. After Captain Colville of HMS *Niger* had successfully wiped out the pirate nest at Tsoo Chong, he wrote to Rear-Admiral Sir Michael Seymour, his Commander in Chief, and said: 'Yet to Mr Caldwell the success attending this expedition is mainly owing; without his experience and adept method of getting information, I fear our endeavours would have been futile.'

The secret of Caldwell's success was that he could speak fluent Chinese. This made him almost unique in the small European community and practically indispensable to the colonial government.

The Hong Kong Police knew that Ma Chow Wong was wanted in China for piracy. He had organized a raid on his home village of Namtow, where he had been born and brought up. The pirate raid had been a catastrophic failure. Ma Chow Wong had bribed a number of vagabonds to open the village gates for him, but the wind changed at the last moment and his ships were becalmed. His pirates arrived late and, the element of surprise being lost, they were slaughtered by the village 'braves'. Ma Chow Wong was saved from being handed over to the Chinese authorities because of the Arrow War, which was going on at the time. 'Ma Chow' means 'horse grass' in Chinese and Wong had acquired this nickname because he had made a living in his youth as a horse fodder salesman, before he went into the wet fish business. Ironically, Caldwell preferred to call him 'Honest Jack'.

Eli Boggs languished in Victoria Gaol until 1860, when at last an American ship's captain could be persuaded to give the dangerous pirate a passage back to the United States. He spent his time writing poetry. In one of his poems entitled 'Hong Kong: a Gaol Ditty', he states his case:

> 'With pirate fleets sailing round her,
> And extortioners living on shore,
> Who'll grant you a licence to plunder,
> If you're willing to fee them galore.'

In a later verse he predicts that Hong Kong will be destroyed by an earthquake. The legend of his death is told by Captain Augustus F. Lindley, a British mercenary soldier who fought for the rebels in the Taiping Rebellion against 'Chinese' Gordon and his 'Ever Victorious Army', in his childrens' book *A Cruise in Chinese Waters*. His description of Boggs is very different from that of Wingrove Cooke. The 'large lustrous eyes' have

*Hong Kong Island from Kowloon. From a painting by
Thomas Allom based on a sketch by Captain Stoddart RN, c. 1843.*

Distressful Bread 51

become 'stormy, hollow and immovable—as one might imagine the eyes of a dead serpent, only they seemed, somehow, like the slight covering of a hidden volcano' and the 'affluent black hair' was now 'long, straight and limp'. Boggs had been put aboard a British ship, the *Imogene*, and spent a week in irons after almost killing the steward. After his release the strange happenings began. Satanic laughter echoed around the ship and soon everyone aboard was convinced that the *Imogene* was haunted. The ghost seemed to have taken up residence in the maintop and the crew became too frightened to go aloft.

Two days out from the Cape of Good Hope, the ship ran into a violent gale. At last the Bay of Table Mountain came into sight and the topsails had to be reefed. The bravest of the crew went fearfully aloft. They had almost finished when the ghost howled above the storm: 'Die! Die! Your life is mine!' This startled the third mate, who lost his footing and fell. On the way down, his body smashed into Eli Boggs, who was on the lee quarter of the main arm. With a sickening thud they hit the deck together. The third mate died instantly, but Boggs lived long enough to land in Cape Town. His only friend, Friday, the black ship's cook, was with him when he died. 'As Friday bent his ear to the dying man's mouth,' Augustus F. Lindley tells us, he just caught the word 'ventriloquist'. So ends the legend of Eli Boggs.

THE CALDWELL CASE

After the successful conviction of Ma Chow Wong, the Attorney General, Thomas Chisholm Anstey, proclaimed that Caldwell was unfit for office and should be dismissed. Caldwell found an unexpected ally in Sir John Bowring, whose personal hatred for Anstey verged on the paranoia. Anstey had rashly accused a number of officials of various misdeeds, often without sufficient evidence. He had also tried to convict Caldwell's friend Dr Bridges, the Acting Colonial Secretary, for taking 'cumshaw' when awarding the opium monopoly.

Dr Bridges was not a full time civil servant. He was a lawyer, who had been co-opted by Bowring into the civil service to fill the post of Colonial Secretary, left vacant by William

Mercer, who was on leave. Bowring had foolishly let him continue with his private practice while working for Government. The unscrupulous Dr Bridges took full advantage of the unorthodox arrangement. In his capacity as a lawyer, he had accepted a retaining fee of $1,000 from Mr Chun Tai-kwong to help him win the opium monopoly. In his capacity as Acting Colonial Secretary he awarded the opium monopoly to Chun. A Commission of Enquiry found Dr Bridges 'at fault', but Bowring unwisely refused to dismiss him.

When Anstey forced the Governor to convene another Commission of Enquiry with Caldwell in the hot seat, Dr Bridges came to Caldwell's rescue. Caldwell was found guilty of four of the nineteen charges brought against him. These established only that he knew Ma Chow Wong and had done business with him, which was common knowledge. Dr Bridges, as Acting Colonial Secretary, had re-framed the other charges so that he would get off. One of Anstey's original charges was that Caldwell owned and managed a brothel. Bridges revised the charge. The new charge was that Caldwell's Chinese sister-in-law managed the brothel. Caldwell was pronounced innocent on a technicality, because it turned out that the lady in question was not related to Caldwell's wife.

The serious charges concerning piracy were dismissed, because the villainous Dr Bridges had arrogantly burned Ma Chow Wong's 'shop books', which contained most of the evidence against Caldwell. This was too much for the editor of the *Friend of China*, William Tarrant, who called it 'a contemptible and damnable trick on the part of the government.'

Anstey was livid. He had been bamboozled and out-manoeuvred and he knew it. Never a temperate man, Anstey screamed invective and used every opportunity to pour abuse on the wretched Governor, Dr Bridges and the devious Caldwell.

It was all too much for Sir John Bowring. He suspended the Attorney-General from office. Explaining his action to the new Secretary of State for the Colonies, Sir Edward Bulwer-Lytton he wrote: 'viz, impetuosity of temper beyond control, credulity in listening to vague accusations, recklessness in preferring, persistence in adhering to repeating disproved averments and perservering malignity towards every opponent who has the misfortune to incur his displeasure.'

Bowring then sued William Tarrant, the editor of the *Friend of China,* for libel. Tarrant, a former ship's steward and civil servant, had been dismissed from a lowly position in government a few years earlier, for accusing the Police Magistrate William Caine's comprador of taking 'cumshaw'. He was an embittered man who took every opportunity to attack the government. His editorials oozed black bile and venom.

Anstey was under suspension, but as a lawyer he was now allowed to take on private clients. The trial is therefore somewhat confusing to follow, with the suspended Attorney-General, Anstey, defending Tarrant against the Acting Attorney-General, John Day. The outcome was that Tarrant was pronounced not guilty, the government had to pay the costs and Dr Bridges resigned. Anstey's master stroke had been to subpoena the Governor, who had hastily taken a long holiday in Manila to avoid appearing as a witness in court.

DENT'S MOTION

Bowring could not have been out of Hong Kong at a worse possible time. Because of his absence, the second reading of his beloved Praya Scheme had to be delayed. This gave the opposition time to get organized.

Many of the Marine Lot holders had, by the slow and surreptitious reclamation from the harbour, been able to double the size of their original lots. One of the features of Bowring's scheme was that the land they had reclaimed from the sea illegally would be returned to the Crown and they would have to pay rent on it.

The two major Hongs who opposed the scheme were Dent & Co and Lindsay & Co. Although their plots were not very large, they were on prime land between Queen's Road Central and what is now Des Voeux Road Central. Their lots were next to each other and occupied the Ice House Street end of the block, where the Landmark is today.

With the Governor hiding out disgracefully in Manila, avoiding having to appear as a witness in the Tarrant libel case, Dent struck with deadly effectiveness. He proposed a motion in the Legislative Council that the Praya Scheme be adjourned *sine die*, or in layman's terms, indefinitely.

The Lieutenant-Governor William Caine, who thought that he should have been made Governor instead of Bowring, and Chief Justice Hulme did not even bother to turn up for the debate. The two Unofficials, as expected, voted for Dent's motion, but to everybody's amazement, so did three government servants. Dent's proposal was carried by six votes to three. It was a *fait accompli*.

The bumbling Chief Magistrate, H.T. Davies, explained that he thought that the money would be better spent on building a waterworks. The Surveyor-General Charles St George Cleverly said, rather unconvincingly, that he had changed his mind; but the most extraordinary vote came from the Colonial Secretary, William Mercer, who had just returned from leave. A Colonial Secretary voting against a Governor in the old days of the British Empire is a bit like the Vice-President of the United States voting against his President—it was unthinkable.

So what inspired this diabolical act of treachery by Bowring's colleagues? It is true that the Governor had made himself so unpopular with the local population and the British Government in Westminster that he had lost much of his credibility, but Bowring had another explanation. He wrote:

'The enormous power and influence of the great Commercial houses of China, when associated directly or indirectly with personal pecuniary advantages which they are able to confer on public officers, who are permitted to be employed and engaged by them, cannot but create a conflict between duties not always compatible.'

He would seem to be accusing his colleagues of corruption. Ironically he had earlier suspended his Attorney-General, Chisholm Anstey, for expressing a similar opinion.

The Praya Scheme was probably doomed anyhow. Palmerston's Liberal government was no longer in power and Lord Derby's Tories, who had opposed the Arrow War, had little sympathy with Bowring for starting it. The waterfront between Arsenal Street and Central was occupied by the Royal Navy and the military and, without the support of Westminster, Bowring had little hope of getting the War Office to part with it.

BOWRINGTON

Battered but unbowed, the tenacious Bowring did not give up easily. As a Liberal, he accepted his defeat by the democratic process in the Legislative Council rather graciously; as an autocrat he bullied a few of the more vulnerable owners of Marine Lots in Wanchai (mainly Chinese), to let him start building his Praya in front of their holdings.

His proposed new town, Bowrington, was little more than a few hundred square yards of reclaimed land in Wanchai, west of Percival Street. It included Bowrington Street and the Bowrington Canal. Over the years Bowrington has slipped into obscurity. The canal has been filled in and the original tow paths have been renamed Canal Road East and Canal Road West. Today Bowring's dream city, his new Jerusalem, is rather a forlorn place. An enormous flyover flies over the site of the Bowrington Canal and Bowrington Street is a humble market lane, selling scraggy chickens, fruit, fish, meat and cheap vegetables. The dominant feature of this picturesque little Wanchai street is a grim greenish-gray and cream edifice of modern construction. It is called 'The Urban Council Bowrington Road Cooked-Food Centre' and, rather appropriately, resembles a lump of grubby, grey beancurd.

THE LABOURS OF HERCULES

In 1859 the British Government sent out Sir Hercules Robinson to replace Bowring or, as Victorian wits put it, to cleanse the Augean Stables. Sir Hercules was a man of action. One of his first moves was to pass an ordinance that prevented government officials from voting against the Governor. He instituted a new Caldwell Enquiry, which resulted in Caldwell being dismissed and Dr Bridges fleeing the Colony. Anstey demanded to be re-instated as Attorney-General, but Robinson would not have it. Tarrant published a vicious article on William Caine, which was timed to appear the day after Caine left Hong Kong for good. Unfortunately, he got his timing wrong and Caine was still in the Colony when it was published. Tarrant was sent to prison again for libel; Caine having cleverly retained all the barristers practising in Hong Kong at the time, leaving Tarrant with the task of defending himself in court. Ahlum opened another baker's shop in Vietnam and George Duddell, a dubious business man with a street in Central named after him, built a 'poison-proof' bakery which was promptly burnt down by Yeh's urban guerillas. Ahlum was later allowed to return to the Colony.

Sir John Bowring returned to England, married again and lived to the ripe old age of eighty. He was an extraordinary man and his sojourn in Hong Kong was just a passing phase in his incredible career. I have been told by one of his descendants that a recent BBC documentary of his life did not mention his governorship of Hong Kong at all. For once the media seems to have treated him kindly. Most of his life he was at constant war with the press. Tarrant was not the only one to suffer. In one libel case against the editor of the *Hongkong Daily Press*, Yorrick Murrow, the defence claimed that it was impossible to bring the Government of Hong Kong into contempt 'because everybody knew it was contemptible'. This ingenious argument failed to convince the jury and Murrow was sent to prison for six months. The British Press joined in the battle. The *Morning Herald* called Bowring: 'An empty-headed, malevolent, lying, political quack' and suggested that he should be put in a pillory 'so long as bystanders threw nothing hard at him'. There is no record of him suing the *Morning Herald*.

Like many so-called 'bad' governors, Bowring's policies generated change and the thankless task of cleaning up the mess was left to stalwarts like Sir Hercules Robinson.

THE YEARS BETWEEN

With the collapse of Bowring's Great Praya Scheme, the opportunity for Wanchai to develop seemed doomed. Any chance of persuading the Army and Navy to relocate had passed. Not only were they determined not to budge, but over a period of years they increased their holdings by buying more land. The area between Wanchai and Central became a vast military cantonment, consisting of Wellington Barracks, Murray Barracks, North Barracks and Victoria Barracks. In 1899 the Navy needed a graving dock for the large China Fleet, where they could repair and maintain their warships.

Governor Sir Henry Blake made a valiant attempt in 1901 to have the proposed Royal Naval Dockyard built at Quarry Bay, in order to prevent the city from being irrevocably split in two by War Office installations. The Admiralty wanted to build the dockyard in Central, which was to be a joint venture between the Royal Navy and the Hong Kong and Whampoa Docks Company. However, the company demanded a nine hundred and ninety-nine year lease and the deal fell through. So the Royal Navy went ahead on its own and built the dockyard. By the turn of the century almost all the land between Murray Road and Arsenal Street belonged to the War Department. At the bottom of Garden Road was Murray Barracks, where the new Hong Kong Park is today, and above it was Victoria Barracks, which stretched up the hill as far as Kennedy Road. Apart from Queen's Road, and later Kennedy Road, there was no way to get to Wanchai directly from Central. This cantonment cum naval base was known as the 'Waist' because it squeezed urban Hong Kong in two, like a corset, with Central at the top and Wanchai and Happy Valley somewhere in the nether regions.

The British Tommies and Bluejackets originally did their drinking and whoring in Tai Ping Shan; but after their officers put Central out of bounds, they exploded into Wanchai. The

Wellington Barracks, c. 1900.

Queen's Road East showing A. Hing's photographic studio on the corner of Arsenal Street, c. 1906.

Reverend John Turner, a Wesleyan minister, described their behaviour in his book *Kwang Tung or Five Years in South China*: 'They drink like fishes, ride around in rickshaws, make the night hideous with their shouts, eat over-ripe fruit from street stalls, are stricken with cholera, and die in a few hours.'

Turner seems to have been prone to exaggeration. Although in the early years of the Colony, cholera and malaria decimated the garrison, by his time things were under control. The records of the 1st Battalion of the Rifle Brigade show that there were no deaths in the regiment in 1894, the year Turner published his book. The only recorded fatality during their time in the colony was that of Pickles, the regimental dog, who had joined the Rifle Brigade in 1886 and served faithfully in Burma and India before dying in 1896. He was buried with full military honours outside the Officer's Mess at Victoria Barracks.

Attached to every large barracks in the East was an army of camp followers. They moved into Wanchai. Ship Street was the brothel area and, in a desperate attempt to prevent the spread of venereal disease, Bowring licensed the brothels and ordered the regular inspection of prostitutes. Before the age of penicillin, syphilis was rampant. However, the idea of having licensed brothels was repugnant to Victorian England. In 1890 the British Contagious Diseases Act, which allowed for the forcible medical examination of prostitutes in garrison towns overseas, was repealed, with the result that by 1897 almost half of the Hong Kong garrison had syphilis.

Wanchai was no longer a fashionable place to live and so most respectable citizens of Hong Kong moved elsewhere.

EAST POINT

At the other end of Wanchai at East Point, which for some inexplicable reason is west of North Point, the godowns and factories of Jardine, Matheson & Co stood on three and a half acres, bought by Captain Morgan at the first Land Sale in 1841. As the years went by Jardines increased their holdings in the area, including a godown that was bought from a Mr Leighton. It is safe to assume that this is the origin of the name of Leighton Road.

Early in the last century, Hong Kong had no coins of its own: British pounds, American dollars, Indian rupees and Chinese copper cash, were commonly used; but the Mexican silver dollar was by far the most widely circulated coin in the Colony. This distressed Governor Sir Hercules Robinson, who proposed that Hong Kong should have its own currency. It was very expensive to transport large amounts of coins from London to Hong Kong, so he suggested that the Colony should establish its own mint.

Robinson left Hong Kong in 1865 for Ceylon. The mint was opened at East Point in April 1866, a month after his successor, Sir Richard Graves Macdonnell, took office. As a license to mint money it was a disaster. The machines could only produce $15,000 worth of coins per day, while an output of $27,000 was needed to cover costs. Consequently the Hong Kong government was unable to make money by making money. After a couple of years the mint was closed and its machinery sold at a loss to the Japanese government for $60,000. Jardines bought the land.

They built a sugar factory on the site, which was north of Kingston Street. They later took over the Oriental Sugar Refinery, which was situated in the Swatow and Amoy Street area. Their enterprise, the China Sugar Refining Company, was in and out of trouble for the next thirty years. In 1900 Emmanuel Rafael Belilios, an entrepreneur, banker and opium dealer, made a takeover bid for the company. Jardines managed to beat off the challenge. Belilios is best known today as the owner of a camel, on which he used to commute to his offices in Central from the Peak. When the Peak Tramway opened the poor animal became despondent and eventually committed suicide by hurling itself off a cliff. Belilios was a man of many interests. He opened a school for little girls, which is still named after him.

To the north of the sugar factory is Kellett Island, named after Admiral Sir Henry Kellett, the Arctic explorer. Although Sir Robert McClure is credited with discovering the North West Passage, it was Kellett who sent Lieutenant Bedford Pim across the ice floes to establish the vital contact with McClure's expedition. Both he and McClure, whose ships were ice-bound, would almost certainly have been able to sail through the passage from different directions when the ice melted the next summer, had they not been ordered to abandon their ships by the commander of the expedition, Sir Edward Belcher, who years earlier had raised the Union Jack over Hong Kong. When the ice melted, Kellett's ship, HMS *Resolute*, drifted unmanned, like the ghostly *Marie Celeste*, for 1,200 miles through the Davis Strait.

'She must, at first, have looked like a phantom ship', wrote Captain James Buddington of the American whaler *George Henry*, 'a spirit of some ocean child risen from the deep and stalking forth upon the sea, still wrapped in its white grave-clothes.'

Buddington and his crew boarded Kellett's ship and took her back to New London. She was bought by the United States Congress, refitted and returned to Queen Victoria. Years later, when the ship was broken up, a desk was made from her timbers and presented to Congress. It languished in a storeroom at the White House until rescued by President John F. Kennedy

Jardines' Sugar Factory at East Point, c. 1905.

Victoria Harbour before the Praya East Reclamation.

who put it in the Oval Office. The next American President to the use the desk was Bill Clinton. Kellett charted the waters of Hong Kong in the 1840s in HMS *Plover* and thirty years later he returned to Hong Kong as Commander-in-Chief of the China Station. Today Kellett Island is no longer an island, but the home of the Royal Hong Kong Yacht Club.

South of the sugar factory, on Great George Street, stood the Hongkong Ice Company's works. In the early days ice was imported from America by sailing ships and sold at five cents per pound; but in 1874 two enterprising young Scotsman, John Kyle and William Bain, opened a factory to manufacture ice. Five years later they sold out to Jardine, Matheson & Co. The ice company was eventually absorbed by the Dairy Farm Company. Next door was a distillery. Many of the streets in this area are named after Jardine's Taipans: Jardine's Bazaar, Matheson Street, Paterson Street and Percival Street. Alexander Perceval was a relation of the Jardine family by marriage, but he actually spelled his name 'Perceval', not 'Percival'. The mistake was probably the fault of one of Hong Kong's dyslexic signwriters, of which there were many, who were also responsible for painting the 'W' upside down in Wong Kok, thus creating Mong Kok, and spelling 'Alexander' backwards, resulting in the curiously named Rednaxela Terrace.

Near the barracks there are three other streets named after Jardine Taipans: Gresson Street, Anton Street and Langdale Street. Jardine, Matheson & Co had earlier illegally erected some godowns in the area, before the first Land Sale. They were kicked out by Major-General Lord Saltoun, who wanted the land for military purposes. Jardines were paid $25,000 in compensation for the buildings they had erected. This created the curious practice of paying squatters compensation for building illegal structures on Crown Land, an anomaly which is still with us today.

Every day Jardine, Matheson & Co still makes itself heard at East Point, when the boom of its famous Noon Day Gun signals midday. Legend has it that, sometime during the last century, Jardines fired a 21-gun salute to herald the return of one of their Taipans to Hong Kong. As merchant princes are not entitled to 21-gun salutes, this was regarded at the time as an outrageous and unacceptable breach of protocol. As a punishment for their arrogance, Jardines were ordered to fire off a gun every day, exactly at noon, to signal midday. However, Noon Day Guns are not unique to Hong Kong: they have one in St Petersberg and in Quebec they not only have one at noon, but another in the evening as well. In the last century not everybody owned a watch and the purpose of an evening gun was a signal to the troops of the garrison that it was time to return to barracks. In Hong Kong a gun was also fired to announce the approach of a typhoon; a further two rounds were fired when the typhoon was about to hit the Colony. The playwright Sir Noel Coward immortalized the Noon Day Gun in his famous song *Mad Dogs and Englishmen*:

> 'In Hong Kong
> They strike a gong
> And fire off a noonday gun
> To reprimand each inmate
> Who's in late.'

Coward was actually one of the privileged few who has been invited to fire the gun himself. Unfortunately, he was late for the event: on 20 March 1968 the midday signal boomed out over East Point at exactly three minutes past the hour.

EARLY INDUSTRY

Captain John Lamont was probably Wanchai's first industrialist. In February 1843 SS *Celestial*, eighty tons, was launched from his patent slip at East Point. It was the first European ship to be built in Hong Kong. With his partner, Douglas Lapraik, a Scottish watchmaker, he constructed Hong Kong's first dry dock at Aberdeen.

There is always a certain amount of confusion about his neighbour, John Cowper, who also owned a shipyard at Spring Gardens. This is because his name was often misspelled 'Couper' in the old records, possibly because it was pronounced 'Cooper'. Cowper is one of those tiresome British surnames which are pronounced differently from the way they are spelled: like Keswick, Chomondeley and Fetherstonehaugh, only not nearly so distinguished.

John Cowper was originally a carpenter with P&O. After a few years in China he saved enough money to lease the Whampoa Mud Docks from its Chinese owners. He made a fortune. In 1856, during the phoney period of the Arrow War, when Commissioner Yeh was offering money for European heads, he was kidnapped from his ship in the harbour. A contemporary newspaper account tells how it happened:

'On Saturday evening, a little before sundown, a sampan pulled alongside the chop and a man held up a piece of paper pretending that it was a note for Mr Cowper. His eldest daughter went out to receive it but the Chinese refused to give it to anyone but Mr Cowper and he thereupon stepped down the gangway. When in the act of putting out his hand for the note, he was suddenly seized by three men and dragged into the sampan. His daughter held on to his coat for some time and would have succeeded in rescuing him had he not slipped overboard whence he was lifted into the sampan: there he struggled manfully with the six Chinese in the boat and again

The Years Between

jumped in the water—was again picked up and ultimately overpowered and carried off. Despite the alarm which was immediately given and pursuit made by boats in the vicinity, his kidnappers escaped and nothing was afterwards ascertained of him.'

His son offered a reward of $2,000, but John Cowper was never seen again. He was sixty-five years old at the time. His dock at Whampoa was destroyed by a mob a month later. After the Arrow War his son, who was also called John Cowper, received $120,000 in compensation. He rebuilt the Whampoa Docks. After a series of complicated mergers involving the shipyards owned by Captain Lamont, Douglas Lapraik and others, his old firm became known as the Hong Kong and Whampoa Docks Company. Its first chairman was Sir Thomas Sutherland, the P&O agent, who was the driving force behind the creation of the Hongkong & Shanghai Bank. After reading a number of articles in Blackwood's Magazine on banking, on a boat trip between Hong Kong and Foochow, Sutherland came to the conclusion 'that one of the simplest things in the world was to start a bank in China'...and did it. In later years he was fond of saying: 'I never had a banking account in my life; I had only an account with a compradore which was generally overdrawn.'

There were other shipyards in the area. McDonald & Co built gunboats for the Imperial Chinese navy. They launched two warships in 1866, which were registered at a hundred and eighty tons, made from teak and fully coppered with Muntz's metal. Their boilers were manufactured by MacDougall & Co (also of Wanchai). They had eighty horsepower engines. These lethal little schooner-rigged vessels were armed with four 18-pounders and one 24-pounder swivel gun.

There was also an American shipyard, owned by Charles Emery and George Frazer, in the Fenwick Street area. This yard eventually fell into the hands of George Fenwick, who had been an engineering officer aboard HMS *Victor Emmanuel*. His firm, Fenwick & Morrison, was in business from 1881 until 1892. One of Fenwick's former draughtsmen, Lan Fat, owned the Tung Tsai Tseung Kee & Co, which had a workshop at Praya East and employed five hundred workmen. He also

The Pak Tai Temple with the Naval Hospital in the background, c. 1890.

Wanchai shopkeepers stock up with lanterns for the Mid-Autumn Festival.

had a firm in Manila, which built over a hundred launches, and another in Saigon, which had a contract with the French Government.

A Tan, who had offices at 63-65 Queen's Road East, was a master builder of considerable skill. He specialized in military contracts and built the Gun Club Hill Barracks, Kennedy Road Married Quarters and the Jubilee Hospital on the Peak. He also built the Foo Moon Forts in Canton and was made a mandarin.

Apart from shipyards, there were sailmakers, boilermakers, engineering works and dozens of ships' chandlers. Near the barracks there were military tailors, tattoo artists, curio shops, pawnbrokers and A Hing's photographic studio. There was Morgan's Bazaar, which Captain Morgan set up in competition to the Canton Bazaar, and there were markets and a proliferation of hawker stalls. There was a steam laundry at Bowrington Canal. Nearby, Weisman's foreign bakery sold plump croissants, pretzels and pumpernickel, which tempted the inhabitants of the more fashionable Mid-Levels to drive down in their carriages to Wanchai to do their shopping. A century later, Wanchai is still one of the most popular shopping areas in Hong Kong.

CHURCHES, TEMPLES AND OLD BUILDINGS

In the early 1840s there was a large Roman Catholic community living in the St Francis Street area, close to the first Catholic Cemetery. They worshipped at St Francis Chapel. Close by was St Joseph's Hospital, a Mission House and a school. In 1849 a number of houses were built for the poor on the land between the Catholic and Protestant cemeteries. There was an orphanage just down the road, between Anton Street and Li Chit Street, called Asile des Sainte Enfrance, which was run by the French Sisters of St Paul de Chartres, who arrived in the colony in 1848. Sir Paul Chater bought the land in 1906 and the nuns moved to Happy Valley. There is still a strong Roman Catholic presence to be seen in the St Francis area today, including the Lok Kan School, operated by Caritas, and Our Lady of Mount Carmel Church. In the last century it was very much a Catholic enclave, inhabited by poor Portuguese, Goan and Chinese Christians. The Protestants, in the form of the

London Missionary Society, had a chapel in the Wanchai Road, near their preserve at Morrison Hill.

THE HUNG SHING TEMPLE

Probably the earliest religious building in Wanchai is the Hung Shing Temple on Queen's Road East, which was built in 1860. There is a shrine at the rear of the building that bears an inscription dating back to 1847. It is thought that there was an even earlier shrine on this site and possibly a small fishing community living nearby. When the temple was built, it stood on the waterfront. This is appropriate, as legend has it that Hung Shing was the reincarnation of the Dragon King who ruled the southern seas. His speciality was suppression of 'all monsters and phantoms inimical to those whose business is dependent on their waters'. A more credible legend is that he was the Tang Dynasty Governor of Kuan Li, an ancient astronomer who issued weather forecasts, thus pre-empting the Royal Observatory by a thousand years. His spirit is said to carry on the good work today by saving seafarers from typhoons and other natural disasters.

THE PAK KUNG SHRINE

This can be found at 7 Star Street. It is a small earth god altar and is said to be about ninety years old. The shrine is protected by a corrugated iron roof of more modern construction. Every village has an earth god. Like tree gods and household gods, these deities were around before the advent of Taoism, Buddhism, Confucianism and ancestor worship. They are said to date back to Neolithic times. Their shrines are generally tiny and often little more than a hole in the wall or a stone with a few joss sticks in a tin can smouldering in front of it.

THE PAK TAI TEMPLE

This Ching Dynasty temple is called Yuk Hui Kung and was built in 1863. It is in Stone Nullah Lane. There is a bronze idol of Pak Tai, which is dated 1604. Pak Tai is also known as the 'Spirit of the North'. He is Taoist divinity who is popular with seafarers, although his connection with water is somewhat tenuous. The folk historian V.R. Burkhardt tells us that when he was a child 'he had an aversion to water when used for ablutionary purposes'. One day he demanded a bath. After he had scrubbed himself clean he forbade his aunt to throw out the bath water, but as 'the greyness of the liquid bore evidence of the desirability of the cleansing process', the old lady slung the lot into the street. Overnight the dirty water was transmuted into gold and her nephew was 'translated into paradise'. The gold was intended to provide for his aunt in her old age, but most of it was purloined by her greedy neighbours. Pak Tai is worshipped by many as a God of Wealth; consequently he is very popular in Hong Kong today.

LIN FA KUNG TEMPLE

In Tai Hang, which is now in the Wanchai District, there is the old Lin Fa Kung Temple. It was built in 1864 and dedicated to the Goddess of Mercy, Kuan Yin. The architecture of this temple is quite unique.

There used to be a tiny temple on Queen's Road East, which has been demolished. It stood next door to the old Wanchai Post Office, which was built in 1912, and now houses the Environmental Resources Centre. The first American resident in Hong Kong, Charles Van Megan Gillespie, who arrived in the colony in 1842, built a splendid mansion on the site at a cost of $2,800. It was called Jorrock's Hall. Gillespie had an office over the road in the Albany Godown, which was later occupied by the army and renamed McGregor's Barracks, which is how McGregor Street got its name. Gillespie, who sold everything 'from a sheet anchor to a skupper nail—a penny whistle to a German flute', got into financial difficulties and the Governor, Sir Henry Pottinger, would not let him leave Hong Kong until he had paid his debts. He sold Jorrocks Hall, which was demolished and replaced by a Police Station, before becoming the Post Office. There were a number of army and naval institutions, church missions and clubs in Wanchai. The

The Lin Fa Kung Temple, dedicated to the Goddess of Mercy Kuan Yin.

largest was the Royal Naval Canteen, which was known as the Blue Buildings, the forerunner of the China Fleet Club, which stood at the Central end of Praya East, approximately where Johnston Road begins today.

THE EARLY POPULATION

The governors, taipans and judges may have moved elsewhere but there were still plenty of Europeans living in Wanchai. The shipyards, sugarworks, power station, tramways and docks all employed skilled workers and, as there was virtually no public transport until the tramway was opened in 1904, apart from sedan chairs and rickshaws, the less affluent tended to live close to their places of employment. The number of Europeans living in, or near, Wanchai was considerable when compared with the European population as a whole. For instance, Captain Lamont employed at East Point: G. Humphrey (superintendent engineer), John Jack (carpenter), James McConnachie (blacksmith), George Ironside (bookkeeper), M. McFarlane (clerk). Most of the other shipyards and godowns, including Jardines at East Point, had a number of European staff. Added to this there were the married soldiers from the barracks and their families, guards from the Naval Dockyard and policemen, who were often quartered in Wanchai. Wanchai became a small European working class area.

The Chinese inhabitants were mainly shopkeepers, small businessmen and artisans, who tended to live on the premises. The coolies either lived in doss houses or in squatter huts in the nearby countryside on the outskirts of the city. Like any maritime area of a large port city in the East, there was a large transient population of discharged sailors, deserters, beachcombers, vagrants, vagabonds, derelicts and drunks. There were a number of small hotels and cheap boarding houses.

Bill Lewis, a well known pugilist, lived for many years in Dick Whittaker's Praya East Hotel. Whittaker, who was a sports promoter as well as a publican, also owned the old Victoria Hotel at 1 Queen's Road East. When he applied for 'a licence to sell by retail intoxicating liquors', his application was rejected by the magistrates. 'Old Colonial', writing in the *South China Morning Post*, explains why: 'They wished it understood that they had nothing against Mr Whittaker, but they objected to the locality.' The Victoria Hotel was too close to the Barracks.

Before World War Two Hong Kong was a snob-ridden society, even though attempts to establish a British class system were not particularly successful. Apart from the odd aristocratic military or naval officer, like Captain Elliot and Lord Saltoun, there was virtually no hereditary upper class. The younger sons of the aristocracy tended to prefer the more prestigious Indian Civil Service, leaving Hong Kong to be run by the Scottish and Irish middle classes. Consequently everybody moved up a couple of notches in the social scale: people like Captain Lamont, who started life as a ship's carpenter, or his colleague Douglas Lapraik, who was originally a humble watchmaker's apprentice in D'Aguilar Street, ended up owning shipping lines and docks. Lapraik built himself a castle at Pok Fu Lam, which today is used as a hostel for Hong Kong University students.

However, the colony was riddled with social cliques and the wives of the European artisans in Wanchai were not invited very often to take tea with the wives of the taipans, who would probably have been dismissed as mere 'box wallahs' by polite society in British India. Hong Kong in the last century was a place of opportunity, as it is today.

As Professor H.J. Lethbridge points out, in his extensive essay entitled *Condition of the European Working Class in Nineteenth Century Hong Kong*, that almost nothing was written about them and the working class 'were not inclined to record on paper their thoughts and experiences for posterity'. Unfortunately, about the only thing to be gleaned from the old newspapers about Wanchai is that a hundred years before Andley Chan, 'The Tiger of Wanchai', got himself shot at the Macau Grand Prix, Wanchai had a crime problem.

THE BATTLE OF GRESSON STREET

Most of the crime in early Wanchai was confined to mugging drunken sailors, burglary, extortion and petty theft, but there was one spectacular shootout which took place during World War One.

'The Battle of Gresson Street' has often been compared with 'The Siege of Sydney Street', when Winston Churchill, aided by Metropolitan Police and the Scots Guards, fought a ferocious gun battle with 'Peter the Painter' and his Russian anarchists. Sydney Street is in London's East End.

On 22 January 1918, a party of unarmed police officers under Inspector O'Sullivan and Sergeant Clarke entered 6 Gresson Street in search of stolen property. They were met by a hail of lead. O'Sullivan and Clarke were shot dead; PCs Sun Tai, So Kai and Kwong Sang were all wounded.

Inspector Sim, the commander of Wanchai Police Station, happened to be passing Gresson Street at the time and had just spotted a body lying on the pavement, when a Chinese detective rushed up and told him what had happened. He telephoned for help and soon the police arrived in force. One party under, Sergeant McWalter, climbed on to the roof of 13 Lun Fat Street. They saw three robbers burst out of the

A typical group of Chinese tradesmen and artisans, 1912.

house and opened fire. The gunmen retaliated and shot PC Tang Wui in the arm. Two of the robbers were cut off by Inspector Sim and a couple of Indian Police Constables in Lun Fat Street. The robbers opened fire—and missed. Sim blasted off five shots. His revolver jammed. The robbers ran down to Queen's Road East and up into Ship Street, hotly pursued by Sim and his party.

One of the desperados, who had a pistol in either hand and one clenched between his teeth, managed to escape after killing PC Mullah Singh and wounding PC Tana Singh. The other ran into Hill Terrace.

Sergeant 'Kid' Marriott of the Royal Naval Police and his wife, who lived nearby, rushed to the window to see what was happening. They spotted a robber climbing up a drainpipe. He shot at Mrs Marriott and missed. The 'Kid' grabbed his service rifle and shot him dead. The robber was found to have four revolvers tied to his wrist by a piece of tape.

Sir Henry May, the Governor of Hong Kong and a former Captain Superintendent of Police, arrived on the scene with Major Robertson of the Army Ordinance Corps and other military officers. They were met by Sergeant Wills, who had just been shot in the leg. A Chinese police constable, who had taken off his uniform jacket, was mistaken for a robber and just missed being slaughtered by friendly fire.

The siege of Gresson Street lasted for eighteen hours. It ended when Major Robertson hurled a smoke bomb through the window and the police stormed the building. They found only one robber inside the house, who had shot himself in an attempt to commit suicide. He later died in hospital. Three of the gunmen were killed and three managed to escape. Four policemen lost their lives and six were wounded.

But who were the gunmen? The police thought that they were Northern Chinese by their features and the way they were

Dockyard foremen, engineers and craftsmen, 1912.

dressed. They all had gold cuff links and natty fob watches and wore identical blue European suits and short fur-lined coats. The *Hongkong Telegraph* had its own theory as to who they were: 'From all appearances they seem to belong to the class which are commonly seen going through the streets doing conjuring tricks.'

THE PRAYA EAST RECLAMATION SCHEME

In 1920 the Public Works Department drew up plans to reclaim 2,249,000 square feet from the harbour. At the time, the road that ran along the sea wall was called Praya East. It started at the Royal Navy Arsenal Yard, at Arsenal Street, and ran along what is now Johnston Road to Stewart Road; from there is continued along today's Hennessy Road, past Bowrington, to Percival Street. There was a small area of land that had already been reclaimed north of the Praya, between Spring Gardens and Wanchai Road, where No 2 Police Station had been built.

The engineer in charge of the Praya East Reclamation Works, John Duncan, had a simple plan. Build a sea wall along today's Gloucester Road; knock down Morrison Hill and use the earth to fill in the hole. The *China Mail* explains:

'Imagine for a moment Hongkong's 'Finest Site' surmounted by a column of earth rising nearly a mile high in the air and you will have some conception of the amount of soil to be torn from Morrison Hill and thrown into the harbour under the Praya East reclamation scheme - the most costly venture yet fathered by the local public works department.'

The problem was how to get the earth to the site without disrupting the traffic. To do this Duncan built a special railway, which ran under the bridge at Bowrington Canal. It was six feet above the water level at low tide. Over the bridge ran the existing tramtrack, which made it impossible to raise the bridge, so at high tide the railway was under three feet of water. The trucks were taken to one side of the canal by one locomotive and changed trains in midstream. They were coupled to a second locomotive on the harbour side. The *Far Eastern Economic Review* explains: 'Scientific shunting on both sides of the bridge will ensure that the trucks are handled with minimum delay.' Four locomotives, fifty Decauville wagons and a hundred side-tipping trucks were used. Work began in 1922 and the reclamation took six years to complete.

WHAT'S IN A NAME

There is speculation that the selection of street names on the new Praya East Reclamation was chosen by a government committee. This is because most of them were named after high-ranking Hong Kong civil servants. One of the exceptions is Gloucester Road, which gets its name from the Duke of Gloucester, not the evil Richard Crouchback who smothered the little princes in the Tower, but Prince Henry, who was the son of King George V and was at one time the Governor General of Australia. During the Japanese occupation, the name of Gloucester Road was changed to Higashisumi-Yoshi-Dori. Strangely, there seem to be only two other streets in Wanchai to be given Japanese names at that time; they were Queen's Road East, which became Higashi-Mesi-Dori, and Yee Wo Street, which was called Kasuga-Dori. It is quite understandable that the Japanese were reluctant to have a street named after Queen Victoria or Prince Henry, but why they changed the name of Yee Wo Street is a mystery. Yee Wo, which is spelled 'Ewo' almost everywhere else, was an alternative name for Jardine, Matheson & Co. In the early days in Canton, Jardines were closely associated with a Chinese merchant called Howqua, whose trade name was Ewo. Jardines also owned the Ewo Shanghai Brewery, which brewed the best beer East of Suez before the war. Of course, the change might have something to do with Jardines being called the 'Princely Hong', but perhaps this is stretching credibility too far.

Anyone who thinks that Jaffe Road has anything to do with plump, juicy, succulent, sun-kissed oranges is sadly mistaken. Daniel Jaffe was employed by the Public Works Department and was the engineer in charge of Tai Tam Reservoir.

Sir James Haldane Stewart Lockhart was one of Hong Kong's most celebrated Colonial Secretaries, who later became Commissioner of Weihaiwei, Britain's other enclave in China.

The Royal Naval Canteen was known as the Blue Building and was the forerunner of the China Fleet Club.

Blue Buildings - Praya East, Hongkong.

He was a brilliant Chinese scholar and an exceptionally capable public servant. When Lockhart left Weihaiwei, in 1921, he was presented with a vase of pure water, symbolizing the purity of his administration; the significance of this gift is not always fully appreciated in the girlie bars and massage parlours of Lockhart Road, which carries his name.

For forty-seven years not a street, not a road, not a public building, not even a humble kindergarten was named after Sir John Pope Hennessy, who left Hong Kong in 1882. This was because he was probably the most unpopular governor who ever administered the colony, with the possible exception of Lieutenant General Rensuke Isogai and Lieutenant General Hisakazu Tanaka, whose names are not immortalized anywhere in the territory.

Sir John was a quarrelsome, colourful, eccentric Irishman whose ideas were either ahead of his time or, sadly, a long way behind them. On the positive side, he appointed Ng Choi

Soldiers of the British Garrison, 1910.

to be the first Chinese to serve on the Legislative Council. On the negative side, he stopped building reservoirs because, he claimed, 'they were against Chinese tradition'. He was also strongly opposed to the introduction of flush toilets into the Colony. Unfortunately he is best known for his attempt to horsewhip a puisne Judge with his umbrella, whom he had caught showing an illustrated catalogue of the Museo Barbonica to Lady Hennessy in her boudoir. It contained a number of engravings of classical nude statues and was condemned by Sir John as a 'dirty book'. The Judge got the better of the encounter and triumphantly carried off Hennessy's umbrella, which he hung as a trophy above his mantelpiece. The character of Phineas Finn in Anthony Trollope's novel of that name is supposed to be based on Sir John Pope Hennessy.

Thomson Road, like Jaffe Road, was not in the original street plan of Wanchai. These streets were an afterthought and not gazetted until 1931, two years after the other streets on the new reclamation. Alexander Macdonald Thomson was a Colonial Treasurer.

Johnston Road gets its name from Sir Reginald Johnston, the last Commissioner of Weihaiwei, who had the responsibility of returning the territory to the Chinese in 1930. The British had intended to give the enclave back to China in 1924, but, because of Feng Yu-hsiang's coup d'état, there was no Chinese government to give it back to. Feng was known as the 'Christian General' and used to baptize regiments of soldiers with a fire hose. Johnston, who was the Manchu Emperor Pu Yi's tutor, rescued him from the clutches of the flamboyant Christian General. The actor Peter O'Toole played the part of Johnston in the film *The Last Emperor*.

Luard Road probably gets its name from Major-General C.C. Luard, who was GOC British troops in China at the time of the reclamation. Colonial secretaries Sir Francis Fleming, Sir William Marsh and Sir Frederick Stewart all have their streets. Another Colonial Secretary, Sir Thomas Southorn, whose main claim to fame was that he was married to the sister-in-law of novelist Virginia Woolf, has a playground named after him. The odd man out was Malcolm Straun Tonnochy, who was the Superintendent of Victoria Gaol. Consequently, the Tonnochy Ballroom is indirectly named after an Irish screw.

THE THIRTIES

Most of the new buildings on the reclamation were similar. They were three or four storeys high, overhanging a cloistered pavement that sheltered passing pedestrians from the rain. The pillars of the colonnade were square and the names of the shops were often painted in gorgeous characters on the concrete columns, which supported the living quarters above. At ground floor level there was generally an open shopfront; goods of every kind spilled like a colourful cornucopia on to the pavement. Many of the buildings housed small factories with busy artisans sawing, hammering and welding, generally cluttering up the sidewalk. There are still a few of these buildings left in Wanchai, but the numbers get less and less every year. With their exotic street signs, they were delightfully picturesque, if perhaps lacking a bit in architectural merit. After World War Two, an illegal town of squatter huts spread like a grey fungus over the rooftops of these buildings.

The new Wanchai Market, at the corner of the Wanchai Road and Queen's Road East, was built in 1937 and is claimed optimistically to be designed after the manner of the Bauhaus school. However, the architectural style of Wanchai Police Station in Gloucester Road, which stood on the waterfront when it was built in 1932, defies description. At the junction of Johnston Road and Hennessy Road was the Chinese Methodist Church, which dates back to 1937. In spite of being officially protected as a Grade III listed building by the Antiquities Advisory Board, it was demolished in 1994 to make way for a twenty-three storey office block. Built in a mixture of Chinese and Western styles, it was one of the most delightful buildings in Wanchai. It can only be assumed that the elders of the Methodist Church received an offer they could not refuse. It is a pity that they did not heed the words of Jesus Christ when he said: 'Make not my Father's house a house of merchandise.' Rather than casting the money-changers out of the temple, they demolished the temple.

In the Wanchai Distict, as opposed to Wanchai proper, there is the Tung Lin Kok Yuen in Shan Kwong Road, which is a red brick monastary built in 1935. There is also the classical St Margaret's Roman Catholic church in Broadwood Road and a Sikh Temple at the junction of Queen's Road East and Stubbs Road, which dates back to 1933. The Tam Kung Temple in Blue Pool Road comes from an earlier age. It was built in 1901 by the Hakka people.

THE BATTLE FOR WANCHAI

On 8 December 1941, Japan attacked Hong Kong and their army fought its way through the New Territories, forcing the British to withdraw to Hong Kong Island. Ten days later Japanese forces landed on the Island and established beachheads in the North Point and Shau Kei Wan areas. Almost all that now stood between Wanchai and the battle-hardened troops of the Imperial Japanese Army was a tiny unit of the Hong Kong Volunteers, made up of elderly gentlemen who had been given the task of guarding the North Point Power Station against looters.

The 'Hughesiliers', as they were known, were raised at the beginning of World War Two by Lieutenant-Colonel H. Owen Hughes and were commanded by Major J.J. Paterson, a Jardine taipan. The detachment was composed mainly of British businessmen over the age of fifty-five. It was supported by half a dozen Free French, under Captain Jacosta, and a platoon of the Middlesex Regiment. On this brave little force descended the full fury of the Japanese attack.

With bulldog tenacity, the pensioners of Hong Kong's 'Dad's Army' stubbornly stood their ground, beating off wave after wave of fanatical Japanese soldiers. Typical among the defenders was Private Sir Edward

Trams at Queen's Road East, near Arsenal Street.

82 Wanchai

Des Voeux, a nephew of a former governor and the Secretary of the Hong Kong Club. When it was suggested that he make a run for it, Sir Edward replied calmly that he was far too old to go dashing about and that he was quite comfortable where he was. He died at his post.

After eighteen hours of fierce fighting, a few remaining Hughesiliers shot their way out of the power station and withdrew to an overturned bus on King's Road, where five survivors made a heroic last ditch stand. The 'Battle of the Bus' was fought to the last man— Private G.E. Gahagan. He beat off the final Japanese assault single-handed, killing an officer and four men with his last five bullets. Having run out of ammunition, Gahagan was forced to abandon the bus. The road to Wanchai was now open.

The last stand of the Hughesiliers enabled the British to establish a line of defence, which was 2,000 yards further back at Leighton Hill. It was defended by Z Company of the 1st Battalion of the Middlesex Regiment. They were joined by a few survivors from the Power Station, some Indians from the 5/7 Rajputs and a number of Canadians. In Oliver Lindsay's book *The Lasting Honour*, their commander, Captain C.M.M. Man, tells us that Z Company consisted of the Regimental Band and what he described as 'the odds and sods of the Battalion'. It was not the ideal fighting unit —but the Middlesex Regiment were not known as the 'Diehards' for nothing.

Captain Man wrote: 'One of my chief problems was keeping up the men's morale. I was fortunate in their Cockney spirit. I was amazed at the way they never lost their sense of humour. It became obvious that the Japanese were planning a big offensive into the city. To do so, they had to overrun our positions.'

Japanese troops enter Hong Kong, December 1941.

The Diehards managed to beat off several Japanese attacks, but on the 23 December they were ordered to withdraw to a battle line that ran across O'Brien Road; here Captain Man established his headquarters in a Chinese VD clinic. Z Company had only forty men left. From there on it was fierce house to house fighting. Somehow the Diehards managed to hold their line until the bitter end.

Behind them the British commander, Major-General C.M. Maltby, was putting together a second line of defence. Maltby had his headquarters a few hundred yards down the road in a massive underground bunker known as the 'Battle Box', which was demolished a few years ago to make way for Pacific Place. On Christmas Day 1941, Sir Mark Young, the Governor of Hong Kong, and Major-General Maltby passed through the Middlesex lines in Wanchai to surrender the Colony to the Japanese.

THE ANGELS OF WANCHAI

Before World War Two, it was fairly common for a lonely British soldier to establish a relationship with a local Wanchai girl. During the war the courage of these girls was magnificent. They became known as the 'Angels of Wanchai'. Bob Yates, a war veteran explained: 'I was not in the front line at Wanchai, so cannot personally vouch for the truth of the stories, that they took in the wounded and cared for them or that they took them tea, food and other comforts, but I believe in all honesty that these tales are true.'

In a letter to local historian Phillip Bruce, he described how the girls stood on the roadside and wept as the British Prisoners-of-War were marched away by the Japanese. He goes on: 'Later many came to the wire at the Shamshuipo POW camp to throw soap and food to their boyfriends. They took terrific beatings from the Japs but still returned.'

He recalled how one girl was stripped naked by the guards and was stood in front of the wire in full view of the prisoners. Every now and then a guard would molest her, slap her or throw a bucket of water over her—'it was a chilly day'. After five hours she was set free: 'The girl stood there unflinchingly, and took it all, without, in my opinion, losing one scrap of dignity . . . . . I doubt if you'll ever hear anything other than praise for the Wanchai girls from the ordinary British soldier who knew them.'

Another British veteran, Mick Giblin, wrote: 'The real heroes of Hong Kong, for my money, were first the 'Diehards', secondly those beautiful ladies our sweethearts from Wanchai and Nathan Road. During the fighting they carried ammunition and supplies to the Hong Kong defenders. After the surrender they daily risked their life from trigger-happy Jap guards to bring food they could hardly spare to the inmates of Shamshuipo. We always toast these gallant beautiful ladies at our reunions.'

No wonder they were called the 'Angels of Wanchai' by the British soldiers.

The coolies appear to be Indians on this Japanese propaganda leaflet dropped on Hong Kong in 1941, during World War Two.

THE WORLD OF SUZIE WONG

Wanchai recovered rather quickly from the ravages of war. On 9 October 1945, ten thousand people congregated at Southorn Playground for the combined Victory and China National Day celebrations. In a couple of hours almost two million dollars were raised in aid of Madame Chiang Kai-shek's 'New Life Movement'. Major General H.K. Pan made a stirring speech. The parade left the playground led by a bicycle troupe, followed by youths carrying the standards of China, Great Britain, the United States of America, the USSR and France. There were decorated trucks, tableaux, lion dancers, acrobats, Chinese bands and hundreds of banners with dramatic slogans like 'Long Live the Generalissimo' and 'Down with the Axis'. The crowd burst into cheers as British warplanes roared overhead. At the Cenotaph, Rear-Admiral Cecil Harcourt took the salute as the Union Jack and Chinese National flags were raised simultaneously on two specially erected flagstaffs. The band of the Royal Marines played the National Anthems of both countries as HMS *Anson* fired a 17-gun salute. Among those present were Major-General Pan, Admiral Buckmaster of the United States Navy and Lady Mountbatten.

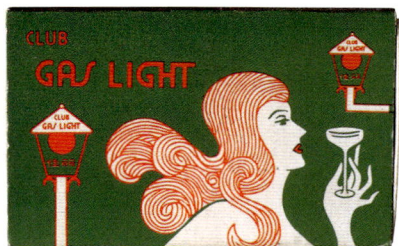

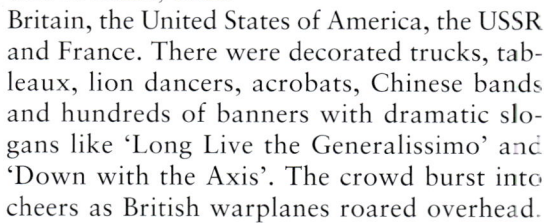

Four days after the Japanese surrender in 1945, a simple four word advertisement appeared in the *South China Morning Post*, it

86 Wanchai

read: 'EAT AT JIMMY'S TODAY'. Wanchai was back in business. Before the war, Aaron Landau's *Jimmy's Kitchen* was a small restaurant in Lockhart Road with wooden tables and bare walls, which specialized in wholesome home cooked meals for British sailors. The restaurant soon had plenty of customers. Larry Allen, Hong Kong's favourite entertainer, dropped in there for a meal just after the war and ordered Steak à la American. This turned out to be steak smothered with tomato ketchup—the ketchup, Larry explained, was American. Jimmy's food is considerably more sophisticated these days. It later moved to Central, but the Landau family still owns one of Wanchai's most popular restaurants, which is appropriately named *Landau's* after the clan.

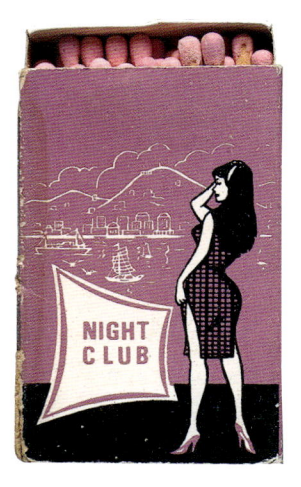

The advantage that Wanchai had over the other districts of Hong Kong was that it was the location of the China Fleet Club, which was the social centre of service life in the Colony. In 1945 the China Fleet Club Theatre became a popular place of entertainment. The British comedian Kenneth Williams made his debut in a review called 'At your Service' and Matt Munroe, the 'Singing Busman', started his career here.

There was soon plenty of other entertainment. In October the White Horse Bar opened in Wanchai and the battered city began to get back to normal. The Café Whoopee offered delicious chop suey and at the Paramount Ballroom hostesses danced with customers (for a small fee) to the dulcet strains of Pinky Pineda and his orchestra. The Plaza Ballroom in Lockhart Road also boasted of a 'galaxy of pretty dance hostesses'.

Hostesses were not a new phenomenon in Wanchai. As long ago as 1851 a merchant seaman complained in a letter to the *Friend of China* newspaper about the behaviour of the girls in a bar called the Seaman's Home:

'They sit uninvited at your table, and are quite ready to share your meal. They can handle a knife and fork, and will take a drink. They chatter away in good English and do not take offence when their 'you like me?' Is turned down with, 'all right, but not tonight".

Before World War Two, girlie bars didn't exist; so the girls hung around outside places like the China Fleet Club, the Soldiers and Sailors Home, the Seaman's Institute, the Nagasaki Joe Hotel and the Black Dog, looking for customers. In his letter, published in Phillip Bruce's *Historical Notes*, veteran Bob Yates explains: "Going Down Home' was the common expression used, so the girl became known as 'The Downhomer', and, depending upon who was being referred to, so was the bloke!'

All this changed following the arrival in Hong Kong of a starry-eyed young novelist called Richard Mason.

RICHARD MASON: THE MAN AND THE MYTH

Apart from a brief period in the middle of the last century during the Arrow War, when the European and Indian communities of Hong Kong were almost wiped out after breakfasting on bread laced with arsenic, Wanchai was little known outside the Colony, except to a few thousand British and American servicemen. In 1957, all that changed with the publication of *The World of Suzie Wong*.

The author Richard Mason was a small literary mystery. No pictures of him appeared on the dust jackets of his novels and, unlike other authors who wrote books with a Hong Kong setting, such as Han Suyin and James Clavell, he was not lionized by the press.

The popular myth, both in Hong Kong and in literary circles in London, was that Richard Mason was a pseudonym and, like John Le Carré and Ian Fleming, he had worked for British Intelligence. Mason's first book *The Wind Cannot Read* is a story of a love affair between a British officer and his Japanese teacher, set in Burma during the war. It was a bestseller.

Even in the 1950s, there was still a tradition that any interracial romance must end with the tragic death of the exotic heroine. Mason used this formula in *The Wind Cannot Read*, where he killed off the beautiful Japanese teacher. In *The Pool*, a short story by W Somerset Maugham, it is the man who dies. Even as far back as Elizabethan times, in Shakespeare's *Othello*, both Desdemona and the Moor of Venice come to a sticky end. Morality seems to have dictated that one or other, or both, of the partners of a mixed-marriage or love affair, had to suffer the death penalty for their indiscretion. However, in *The World of Suzie Wong* Robert Lomax and Suzie not only marry, but there is every indication that they live happily ever after.

There was a story that, after the success of *The Wind Cannot Read*, Mason had planned *The World of Suzie Wong*, chapter by chapter, in London and then came out to Hong Kong, where he carefully selected a bargirl and cynically acted out the plot. The spiteful literati could say anything they wanted to about him, because everybody thought he was dead. He was supposed to have been a fluent Cantonese speaker, who looked like the British film star Anthony Steel, who appeared in *The Dam Busters* and other films of that ilk. Even today, his legendary resemblance to Anthony Steel is an oft-repeated canard.

In 1989 the well-known Hong Kong journalist Ken Barrett tracked down a very-much-alive Richard Mason, who had been living modestly in Rome for some years, shunning publicity. He looked more like Kermit the frog than Anthony Steel and it seems that Richard Mason was his real name after all. He told Barrett that he was the son of an electrician and had been born in Manchester. During the war he was in the Royal Air Force. At the age of nineteen he saw a notice asking for volunteers to learn Japanese. He applied and, much to his delight, spent a year at the School of Oriental Studies in London, where he fell in love with a Japanese girl who was one of his tutors. Mason was posted to Burma, where he wrote *The Wind Cannot Read*. His job was interrogating Japanese prisoners.

When film producer David Lean wanted to make a film of the book, Mason wrote the script. Unfortunately Sir Alexander Korda, who was financing the picture, died and it was eventually made by someone else. As a result, Mason became a screen writer. His next book, *The Shadow of the Peak*, was not a success. In 1955 he had a few months to spare between film assignments, so he bought a ticket to Hong Kong. He told Barrett:

'Arriving in Hong Kong I didn't have much money and I really had no idea what I was going to write about, if anything.

William Holden and Nancy Kwan in Ray Stark's film "The World of Suzie Wong".

I put up at the Luk Kwok. I had no idea of the reputation of the place. It wasn't until later when I went down to the bar, that I realized!'

His room cost him HK$16 a night, which was worth approximately £1 in 1955. Apart from one dinner at Government House, he seems to have spent most of his time at the bar.

'It was fantastic, and I had stumbled right into the middle of it. Never in my life would I find such material again. I just had to sit there eating my fried rice and taking it all in.'

Some years after *Suzie Wong* was published, the *Sunday Times* correspondent Dick Hughes took Ian Fleming to the Luk Kwok bar. Hughes wrote, 'Ian took a reporter's interest in the signs: 'Girls, But No Obligation To Buy Drinks! Take It Easy! You Are At Home! Fine Food And Wines! Enjoy To The Maximum At The Least Expenses!' But he seemed more taken with the Siamese fighting-fish in the huge bowl than with the Suzie Wongs in their cubicles.'

Later, 'purely in a mood of curiosity and investigation', Hughes visited the bar again in the company of his boss, Lord Thomson. They pretended that they were a couple of American paymaster sergeants. Lord Thomson enquired the price of everything. He scribbled down on the back of an envelope a few notes on the cost of 'make lovey' and the hourly price of a room, with or without the company of a bargirl. After a brief chat with the girls, the two old gentlemen left the bar with their chastity still intact.

'We tipped the girls generously and they bowed us out to the door, where the Thomson limousine waited to whisk the pay-master sergeants back to Fenwick Pier and the anchored carrier.' When Hughes asked Lord Thomson if he was thinking of buying the place, the millionaire press baron replied: 'No,

The Queen of the Winner Bar in Luard Road. Silk screen print by Arthur Hacker, 1987.

The World of Suzie Wong 91

but I think I could do worse, don't you think?'

In Mason's book the Luk Kwok is called the Nam Kok. The bar ceased to be a girlie bar thirty years ago. The old building was torn down in 1988 and today there is a magnificent gleaming new Luk Kwok Hotel, which is a model of respectability.

Richard Mason spent only three months in Hong Kong collecting material for his book. It was his first visit to the Colony.

SUZIE WONG: THE BOOK

When Richard Mason started working on his novel he had absolutely no plot in mind. He would sit quietly in the corner of the bar writing. When there were no British or American warships in port and things were quiet, the girls would come over and talk to him and tell him their life stories. The autobiographies of bargirls tend to change with each telling. A lot depended on what film they had seen recently. In Mason's book they seem to have spent a lot of time knitting. It must have been one of those times when the Hong Kong Police, in a periodical fit of morality, had cracked down on gambling in bars. Wanchai bargirls loved to play pontoon. They played by 'Macau Rules', which are difficult to explain except that it was a sure way of losing your money if you were not familiar with them. If an unwary sailor was foolish enough to actually win a game, he was expected to buy a round of drinks. As the stakes were low, his winnings would not cover the cost of the girlie drinks. It was what is known as a 'no-win' situation.

Mason was an excellent scriptwriter and it is the dialogue that makes the book. Nick Demuth, who once lived in the Luk Kwok Hotel and whose band played in the 'Cactus Room' upstairs, maintains that Mason captured the idiomatic English of the girls exactly. He added that, unlike Nancy Kwan, who played Suzie in the film, the Wanchai bargirls of the period tended not to speak with upper class English accents. This observation is true today.

It is difficult to identify with the character of the hero, Robert Lomax, if he can be called a hero, as it takes him a

THE HONG KONG BARGIRL'S PROGRESS

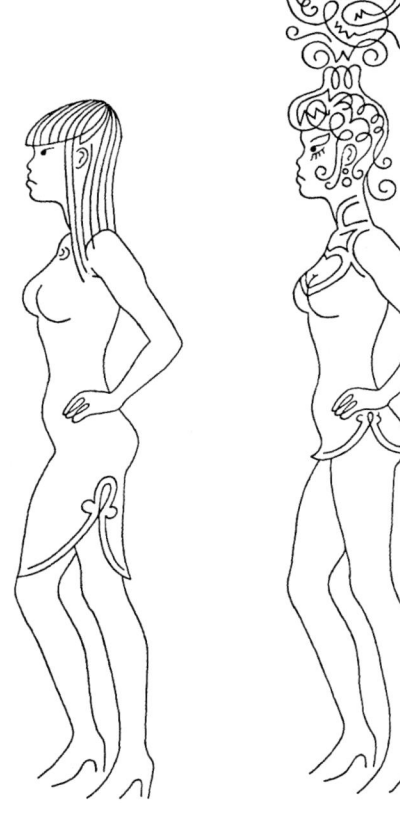

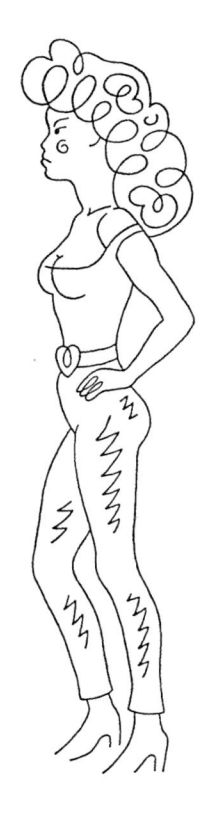

1958
NAME
SUZIE WONG
AGE
18
PROFESSION
BARGIRL
BOY-FRIEND
TOMMY ATKINS
TOP POP SONG
MY OLD MAN'S A DUSTMAN
FAVOURITE EXPRESSION
I LOVE YOU NO SHIT YOU BUY ME DRINK
BEVERAGE
GIRLY DRINK*
HK$5

1968
NAME
MINI WONG
AGE
28
PROFESSION
WAITRESS
BOY-FRIEND
JOE GRUNT
TOP POP SONG
YUMMY, YUMMY, YUMMY, I'VE GOT LOVE IN MY TUMMY
FAVOURITE EXPRESSION
I LOVE YOU NO SHIT YOU BUY ME DRINK
BEVERAGE
WAITRESS DRINK*
HK$10

1978
NAME
OLIVIA NEWTON WONG
AGE
38
PROFESSION
PUBLIC RELATIONS EXECUTIVE
BOY-FRIEND
ABDUL A-BULBUL EMIR
TOP POP SONG
GREASE
FAVOURITE EXPRESSION
I LOVE YOU NO SHIT YOU BUY ME DRINK
BEVERAGE
PUBLIC RELATIONS* EXECUTIVE DRINK
HK$22

1988
NAME
HISPEEDA GONZALES
AGE
18
PROFESSION
DISCO DANCER
BOY-FRIEND
NIPSUBISHI CORPORATION
TOP POP SONG
MONY MONY
FAVOURITE EXPRESSION
I LOVE YOU NO SHIT YOU BUY ME DRINK...SOR'
BEVERAGE
FIRST LADY DRINK*
HK$88

*AN EUPHEMISM FOR A SMALL GLASS OF COLD TEA

Drawing by Arthur Hacker.

The World of Suzie Wong

The collected work of Pinky, the Michelangelo of Jaffe Road, taken in the 1970's.

94 Wanchai

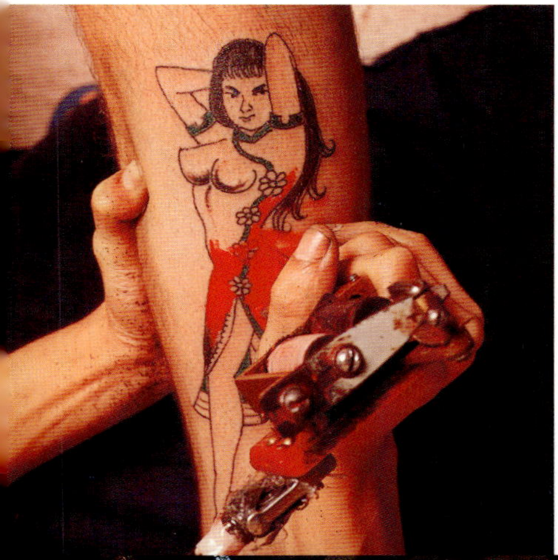

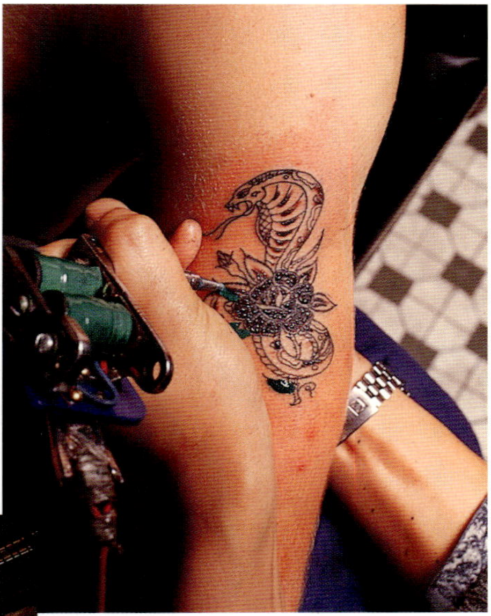

TAURUS
Earth

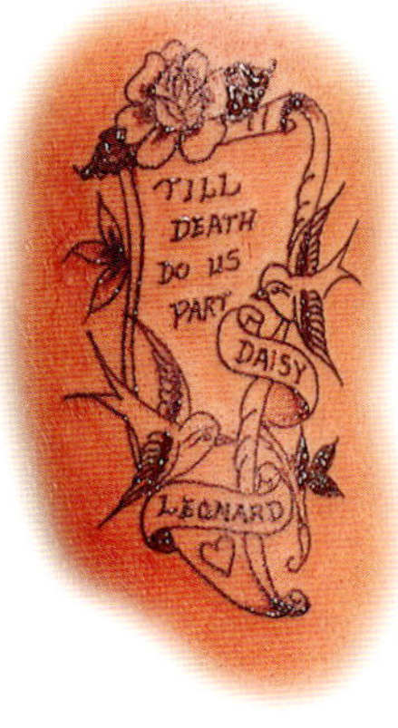
TILL
DEATH
DO US
PART
DAISY
LEONARD

VIRGINIA
HOMEWARD BOUND

hundred and sixty-seven pages before he finally goes to bed with Suzie. In modern fiction he would have made it in the first paragraph, but things were different in the 1950s. The Suzie of the book is far more complex character and far more promiscuous than the Suzie in the film. Her numerous lovers include: a soft spoken Scotsman who gets eaten by a shark; a Hong Kong policeman who fathers her illegitimate child and runs away to Borneo to avoid marrying her; her uncle; an unpleasant neurotic American; a Taipan with an impotence problem; a dirty old coolie; a dozen ancient and decrepit Shanghainese millionaires and two or three thousand American sailors.

Surprisingly few Old Wanchai Hands have actually read the book. Those who are tempted tend to stop at page twenty-nine, when Lomax offers to buy Suzie's best friend Gwenny a drink. Gwenny refuses:

'No, Chinese women don't drink much you know. None of the girls here drink.'

As the whole economy of Wanchai is governed by the number of girlie drinks a bargirl can consume in the shortest possible time, this line is rather unconvincing to the experienced Wanchai wanderer. But perhaps that's the way it was in Mason's time.

In the second half of the book the plot becomes rather contrived. There are a couple of lovers' quarrels and Suzie is sent to gaol for sticking another bargirl between the Bristols with a pair of scissors. Finally even Mason gets fed up and gives her TB, only just when you think he is going to do the traditional thing and have her shuffle off this mortal coil, Suzie recovers and marries Lomax.

'Why didn't you kill her off?' asked Richard Mason's son when he read the book for the first time. According to Ken Barrett, in his article in the *Hong Kong Tatler*, Mason rather regretted that he hadn't had the courage to let Suzie die of consumption. There is a school of thought that maintains it would have been better if he had bumped off Lomax, who is a rather wet young man. However, this would have been rather difficult to do because Lomax is the narrator of the story.

Mason's mastery of dialogue makes his cast come alive, with the exception of Lomax, who is the only unconvincing character in the book. This may be because Mason records Lomax's thoughts as well as his words. In spite of its faults, the novel is an extraordinary record of life in Wanchai in the 1950s, when Hong Kong was a refugee society and when there was real and terrible poverty. It was in an age before credit cards, skyscrapers, unaffordable rents, McDonald's, Vietnam Rose, Super Sandwiches, TVB, ICAC, AIDS and possibly even girlie drinks—if Mason is to be believed. In its own way the book is as much a social history of Wanchai at the time, as Christopher Isherwood's *Goodbye to Berlin* is of Germany in the 1930s.

Suzie Wong must take her place among all the great tarts with golden hearts of twentieth century fiction: Sally Bowles, Sadie Thomson and the delightful Holly Golightly. Without Suzie, Wanchai would be just another urban district of Hong Kong. Suzie gave the place a certain touch of glamour, if perhaps a little tarnished, an identity, an individuality. When Yau Ma Tei, Shau Kei Wan and Tsim Sha Tsui have vanished into the mists of time, the name Wanchai will linger on, simply because Richard Mason made the place immortal when he wrote *The World of Suzie Wong*.

SUZIE WONG: THE PLAY

The play *The World of Suzie Wong* opened at the Prince of Wales Theatre in London in November 1959, with the Shanghai actress Tsai Chin in the leading role. It ran for two years, in spite of being panned by the critics. Bernard Levin called it 'a lot of Chinese junk'. In the 1950s it was fashionable for theatrical critics to write reviews that were self-indulgent little gems, full of twee witticism and clever phrases, which seldom told you anything about the play. The doyen of these ego-trippers was Kenneth Tynan, who, writing about *The Flower Drum Song*, which was playing in the West End at the same time as *Suzie Wong*, damned it as 'The World of Woozy Song'.

Tsai Chin, in her autobiography *Daughter of Shanghai*, tells how the play started a fashion craze:

'Women abandoned the blonde Brigitte Bardot look and grew their hair long and sleek. Some even dyed their hair jet black and pencilled their eyes to be almond shaped. Unfortunately for some, for it was not an easy dress to carry off, the *cheong sam* became the thing to wear.' She added: 'On the gentle curves of a Chinese girl the dress looked sexy but still demure; on Western women with rather more voluptuous proportions the effect was cruder.'

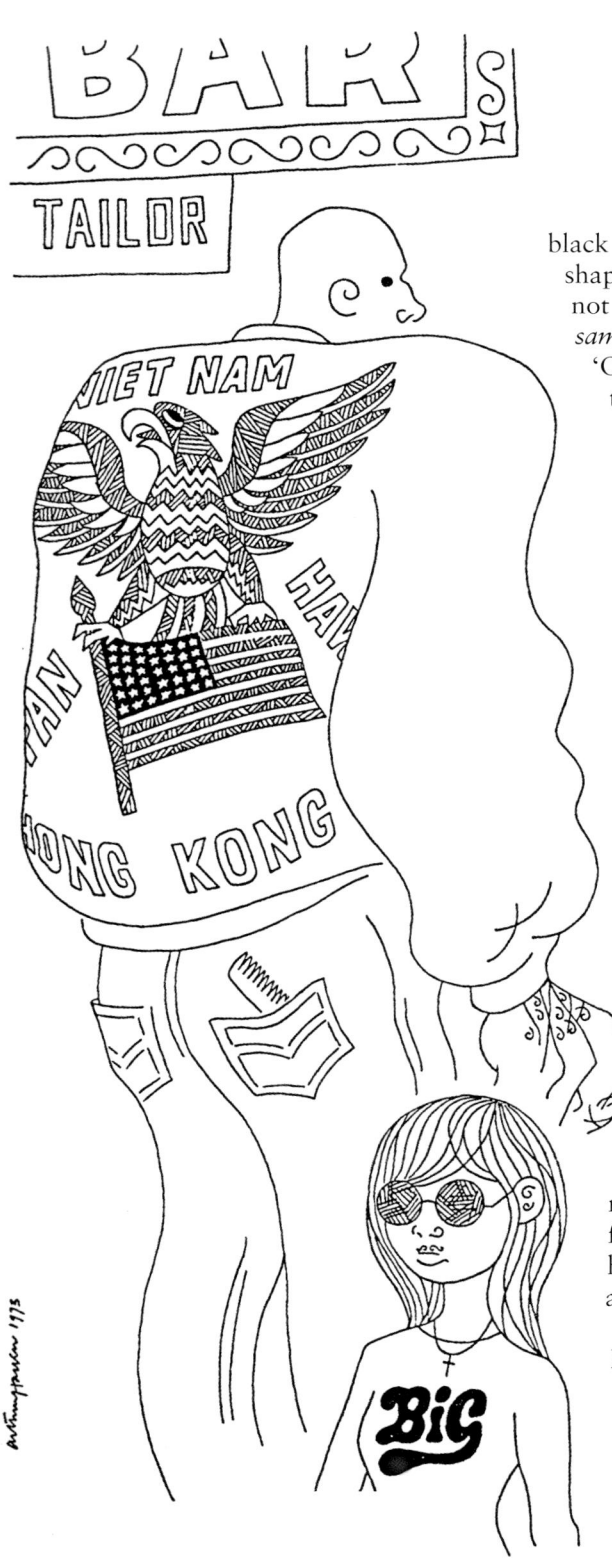

Another product of the play was the 'Ding Dong Song', a Shanghai 1920s golden oldie, which was rearranged by Harry Robertson, with English lyrics by Lionel Bart. It was a hit in the Far East, particularly in the bars of Wanchai, and thousands of pirated records were sold.

The producer of the play, Peter Coe, was a confirmed Sinophile, which is hardly surprising as he was married to the delightful Tsai Chin; but a violent confrontation shattered his rose-tinted spectacles forever, leaving him in a state of post-traumatic stress. Tsai Chin explains what happened:

'Peter still viewed the Chinese as near-saints so he was shocked and hurt when a five-foot tall Chinese waiter hit him on the head with a plate in a restaurant. Peter had refused to pay for a dish which he found unsatisfactory and the waiter had felt the need to express himself across the language barrier.'

The waiter was taken to court. In his summing up the judge said; 'I have always wondered why waiters bring the bill on a plate.'

SUZIE WONG: THE FILM

It is difficult to understand today that making a film with a prostitute as a heroine was a rather daring thing to do in 1960. Of course the French did it fairly often, but it didn't really count because they had a licence to be naughty. Interracial marriages were not considered good box office material at a time when Hollywood was still reeling from the McCarthy Era. Mason's agent was convinced that there was absolutely no chance of the book being turned into a film. However, it was eventually made into a film by Ray Stark in 1960, after MGM and Rank had turned it down.

Nancy Kwan played Suzie and Jacqui Chan, who toured Australia in the title role, played Gwenny. There is no doubt that the two girls stole the show, although expressions like: 'You think me dirty little yum-yum girl!' tended to sound a bit strange when spoken with a Roedean accent and William Holden's portrayal of Lomax was totally unconvincing.

Unfortunately Richard Mason did not write the script and his carefully crafted characters were turned into Hollywood stereotypes. In spite of this the film was a great success and is still entertaining to watch today; but it was not nearly so much fun as the play.

Ray Stark took the position that Hong Kong society would be shocked to the core if a European or American man actually married a bargirl, but in easy-going postwar Hong Kong it was not a particularly unusual event. Couples were not ostracized and there were some very successful marriages: inevitably there were some spectacular failures as well. There was a particularly vivacious bargirl, the uncrowned Queen of the Neptune Bar, who married a fast-talking, wise-cracking American sailor.

Drawings by Arthur Hacker.

They were a swinging couple and all went well until the sailor was discharged from the Navy and took his bride back to his 'ranch' in Oklahoma. The ranch turned out to be a wooden shack with an outside toilet and was twenty-five miles from the nearest jukebox. Her pathetic letters from the dust bowl of America were passed round the bar, much to the hilarity of her friends.

On the whole, Wanchai bargirls tend to make rather good wives and the old Hong Kong saying, 'You can buy a girl out of the bar; but you can't buy the bar out of the girl', has frequently proved to be wrong.

SUZIE WONG: THE GIRL

The immediate effect of the film in Hong Kong was dramatic. Almost every respectable Chinese girl who was called Suzie changed her name. The majority of Chinese girls' English names were not given to them by their parents, but were allocated by their primary school teachers during their first English lesson—and Suzie was one of the most popular. Their Chinese names did not seem to suffer the same fate. Suzie Wong's given name was Mee-ling, the same as Madame Chiang Kai-shek, only the Dragonlady spelled it May-ling.

Dozens of new bars opened in Wanchai, many were named after Mason's heroine; but as a name for a bar Suzie Wong was not as popular as Playboy. At one time there were seven Playboys in Hong Kong and Kowloon and at least two Playgirls, all of which operated in flagrant breach of Hugh Hefner's intellectual copyright. Attempts to persuade the girls to wear bunny costumes were not successful.

Who was the real Suzie Wong? Mason claims that she was a composite character. If there was no genuine Suzie Wong, there were certainly hundreds of phoney ones. During the Vietnam War every bar and nightclub in Hong Kong had at least one girl who called herself Suzie Wong. These girls did not necessarily claim to be the genuine article and some bars had two or three. At the time there were about a hundred girlie bars in Wanchai and three hundred in Tsim Sha Tsui. Added to this there were dozens of dance halls, hostess clubs, massage parlours, illegal barber's shops, music parlours, wankatoria, illegal brothels, night clubs and fish ball stalls. With the odd call girl thrown in, the number of Suzie Wongs must have run into the thousands. The name is not so popular nowadays, possibly because Mason's Suzie Wong would be in her sixties if she were alive today.

One of the most spectacular Suzie Wongs was the Queen of the Pussycat Bar. This long-legged beauty wore fish-net tights and a tiny navy-blue mini-cheong sam, which was cut off in a straight line approximately where the great trochanter joins the ilio-tibial band. This garment had a strategically placed heart-shape cut in the front to reveal just enough cleavage to drive the average red-blooded American sailor, or anyone else for that matter, stark raving bonkers. Pussycat Suzie's *modus operandi* was to prowl just inside the door like a ferocious tigress waiting to ambush her prey. She took not the slightest interest in handsome, musclebound matelots with film star looks, but with precise feline cunning she selected her victims from the most innocent and pathetically inexperienced sailors she could find.

Her skill at extracting girlie drinks from the unwary was legendary. Even Alice the Venus-Drink-Trap could not match her. Girlie drinks in the Pussycat Bar were thimblefuls of cold tea masquerading as hard liquor. Long-legged Suzie drank them at great speed until the poor innocent sailor, who was probably trying to match her drink for drink with hard liquor, fell over blind drunk. Sometimes the poor sailor just ran out of money first and couldn't afford to buy her any more drinks, whereupon Suzie called him a 'Cheapskate Charlie' and flounced off in a contrived huff, her delightful little buttocks twitching viciously. Pussycat Suzie was the doyenne of the Wanchai professional virgin brigade. She never slept with sailors and was rumoured to be married to a policeman.

Professional virgins were not popular with the other girls and Suzie's only friend in the bar was a spectacularly tough-looking harpy known as the Magnificent Ugly, who was always picking fights with Alice the Venus-Drink-Trap. Unfortunately for her, Alice, who looked like a Modigliani waif, packed a vicious left hook. What happened to Pussycat Suzie is not known; perhaps she went the way of all flesh. The Magnificent Ugly got a job on the Stock Exchange and Alice married an American sailor and was last heard of taking a Masters' Degree in Anthropology at Berkeley.

WANCHAI: THE VIETNAM WAR ERA

The late 1960s was probably the heyday of the Suzie Wong Era. Thousands of seamen on Rest and Recreation (R&R) from the Vietnam War roared into Wanchai. Alcohol was not allowed on American warships, so after a couple of a months cooped up in a stinking iron hulk without a drink or female company, mob after mob of sex-starved sailors hit the Wanch with their pockets full of combat pay, a monumental thirst and murder in their trousers—money was no object.

Local cynics would sit quietly at the bar watching the classic confrontation between the avaricious bar girl and the over-eager sailor. Even the most promiscuous bargirl's objective was to get as much money out of the poor sailor, without giving anything in return, particularly sex, which took up a certain amount of time. As well as the standard drink of 'Hong Kong Tea' at ten dollars a shot, there was a phoney pepperminty Crème de Menthe, known as 'Green Slime', which cost $25; and, for the very wealthy, 'Champagne', which was poured brazenly and directly from a freshly-opened bottle of Babycham and sold at the exorbitant cost of $50 a glass. As a Hong Kong dollar was worth about ten times what it is today, girlie drinks cost a lot of money. From a ten dollar drink, the bargirl received four dollars, the bar got four dollars and the mamasan's share was two dollars.

You didn't have to be an expert with an abacus to work out that drinking Green Slime was more profitable than prostitution and far less exhausting. If a girl was bought out of the bar, at a cost of anything from fifty to a hundred dollars, the bar fine went directly to the management. Suzie was allowed to keep anything she made from extra-curricular activities. Many of the bargirls came from desperately poor backgrounds and much of the money went to feeding their families in China or putting younger brothers through college in Canada. Many

American sailors taking happy snaps in Lockhart Road, 1966. Photo Yau Leung.

of Hong Kong's élite owe their start in life to the tireless labours of an elder sister; but poverty was not the only reason why a girl became a bargirl.

In those days there was very little entertainment in Hong Kong for a single girl who had to have fun and sitting at home in a grim, crowded resettlement block watching Cantonese Opera on a black and white television, surrounded by an enormous extended family, was enough to drive any adventurous girl out to the bright lights of Wanchai, with its glitzy glamour and live jazz bands. There were no discos, no Canto Pop and no Karaoke. Big Louie, who ran the Ocean Bar, ably assisted by Diamond Jim, used to hire jazz bands from the US Navy ships. This made the Ocean Bar very popular with the expatriate community, which was equally starved of entertainment. After a dinner at Luigi's Garden, which was the only Italian restaurant in Wanchai (or in Hong Kong for that matter) and was famous for its Shrimp Gumbo Soup, a married couple would spend the rest of the evening in Ocean Bar listening to jazz and chatting to Spring Water, who was everyone's favourite mamasan. If there was a great band they would sometimes take their children along to the 'Naughty Daddy's Club', as a special treat.

There was surprisingly little trouble. The sailors all wore uniform and the girls mini-cheong sams. If a sailor got too drunk he was generally picked up and carried out by his friends or, if things got really out of hand, a quick telephone call brought the Shore Patrol round and the offender was discreetly hit over the head and whisked away. All things considered, there were remarkably few fights.

The Ocean and the Pussycat had as many as a hundred girls working there at any time; whereas smaller bars like the Cave Bar in Luard Road had no more than a dozen and could not afford a live band. It was a popular drinking hole with the press, until the unexpected arrival of a local pop group. They were so bad that they made Sid Vicious sound like Segovia. On their first night a reporter from the *Star* gave them $100 to shut up and go home. This was probably more than the group earned in a week. A couple of nights later the reporter ran out of money. Meanwhile the bandleader had become quite friendly with the press, who found it cheaper to buy him beers, at two dollars a glass, than paying for the band not to play. In the course of conversation they discovered that the bandleader was anxious to find a suitable foreign name to match his talents as a musician and the gentlemen of the press kindly supplied him with one. They even took his photograph. A few days later Hitler Lau's picture graced the entertainment pages of the *Star* newspaper.

THE GENTLEMEN OF THE PRESS

Bargirls and journalists have a lot in common. They are basically lazy, but work very hard for short periods of time. During the Vietnam War there was great influx of young newspaper men into Hong Kong, hoping to make a name as war correspondents in Indo-China. Many of them fell by the wayside and ended up working for local newspapers or magazines. There were only three pubs in Hong Kong at the time, Condor's, Joe's Bar and Fat Eric's, and people tended to drink in clubs or hotel bars, which were rather expensive. Wanchai bars were surprisingly cheaper, if you didn't buy girlie drinks, and the Blue Sky Bar in Jaffe Road was the cheapest of the lot. It became an unofficial press club. It also gave credit and beer was only one dollar and twenty cents a glass, while girlie drinks at four dollars and ninety cents were almost affordable.

The other principal attraction was Brandy Nancy. This splendid lady was more than a congenial drinking companion to the lonely young journalists. She bought them drinks, lent them money, paid their bail and visited them in hospital. She drank her brandy neat—and in large quantities. But woe to the journalist who didn't pay his bar bill on time. The moment his wage packet appeared so did Nancy, who would chase him around his desk, to howls of abuse from his colleagues, until he was shamed into paying his bar bill.

Unlike the bargirls in the big clubs, the Blue Sky girls didn't pester the locals to buy them girlie drinks and only occasionally the classic Wanchai bargirl's war-cry 'I love you no shit! You buy me drink!' was heard across the crowded bar. This would be directed against the odd American sailor who drifted in occasionally by mistake. The Blue Sky Bar was also a favourite with British squaddies and the Americans tended to avoid it for that reason.

Apart from the price of the beer, it was the menu that attracted the British soldiers: Eggs and Chips, Bangers and Mash, Baked Beans on Toast and Fried Rice. If there was a scraggy little chicken scratching around the backyard, you knew that Chicken à la King would soon be added to the bill of fare. The chef, Din Din, who doubled as the lavatory attendant, was a sad-looking old man with a shock of horrent white hair and dead mercenary eyes, which only lit up when he was strangling the unfortunate chicken. He was rumoured to be the retired public executioner from Canton. He did a great job on the chicken.

Almost every bar girl had a nickname: Nature's Child, Dirty Diane, the Golfbag, the Skull and the Splendour That Once Was Maria, all worked in the Blue Sky at one time or another. There was one sweet little girl who claimed to be a virgin and was known rather unkindly as Short-time Alice.

There were two Playboy Clubs in Luard Road in the 1960s.

The girls, of course, had nicknames for the journalists, but most of them are too obscene to print here.

Women journalists also drank at the Blue Sky. There was one particular lady wordsmith, a wild nymphomaniac who swore like a trooper, who was unpopular with the bargirls: 'That girl! She no good! She make "I love you" on the house!'

they would complain indignantly.

When the Blue Sky Bar eventually closed, possibly because the journalists did not pay their bills, they got together and started the Press Club. It was in Luard Road, on the premises of the old Professional Club, which had just gone bankrupt for the same reason. During the Vietnam War, all Wanchai Bars closed at two in the morning, with the exception of the Professional Club and the Professional Musicians Association, which were allowed to stay open all night, because they were allegedly 'professional' organizations. Here you could drink and eat cheaply and there was no adulterated liquor and no girlie drinks. They were haunted by the night people: waiters, barmen, club owners, bargirls, policemen and, of course, the gentlemen of the press, who would drop in for a drink after work. After the licensing hours were lifted and the other Wanchai bars could stay open all night, both these clubs closed.

Why the Press Club never went bankrupt is one of Wanchai's most insoluble mysteries. It is not only in existence today, but is flourishing. Journalists tend to argue whether its finest hour was when the Governor Sir Murray MacLehose dropped in for a beer or the night when the club launched Hong Kong's first streaker into the unfriendly night. The operation was not a success. This was because the streaker, an obese, naked, pink and white Scotsman, ran into a posse of French matelots and fled screaming back into the Press Club to delighted howls of 'Ooh La-La!'

SPIES, SPOOKS AND TATTOOS

Espionage was quite fashionable during the Cultural Revolution. It was the age of James Bond and Hong Kong became known as the Casablanca of the Far East. The expatriate community seemed to be divided between those who everybody thought were spies and those who pretended to be spies. There must have been some genuine secret agents as well, but if there were any they kept well out of sight. In Wanchai it was a distinct advantage to be thought a spook, because you were charged less for a beer in the girlie bars.

At the time it was possible to bargain over the cost of a drink, as there were no fixed prices and much depended on who you were or what you did. Local Chinese were charged the most. This was to keep them away from the bars in order to avoid unnecessary friction between locals and sailors. Black American sailors paid more than white American sailors. Next came tourists, followed by British squaddies, friendly locals, journalists and the police. Spies paid less than everybody else, with the possible exception of racing tipsters, who seldom paid anything at all. There were three sorts of bars in Wanchai, pro-Communist, pro-Kuomintang and those which were loyal to the British Crown. In theory, the pro-British bars were open all the year around, the KMT bars would take a holiday on the Double Tenth and the Communist bars would shut on the first of October, which is China's National Day. Any sensible bar shut its doors on Burns' Night. It became a ritual to visit Wanchai on the first and tenth of October. The game was to try to spot the secret agents surreptitiously going through the laborious task of finding out which bars were open for business and which were not. As there were around a hundred bars in Wanchai, this became an annual excuse for a night on the town. For the record, the Choi brothers' bars: the Ocean, Pussycat, Neptune, Playgirl, two or three Playboys, the Side Door and the Back Door were all shut on the first of October. The Poon brothers' bars: the Washington, Winner Horse, King's and Blue Sky remained open. On the Double Tenth the position was reversed.

What were the secrets the American sailors whispered in the ears of their loved ones in the moment of truth, which were so vital, and who benefited from the information? The answer seems to be the dates the American warships docked in Hong Kong. This information was useful to just about everybody, except perhaps the Viet Cong in their jungle hideouts. Show business magnates knew just when to fly in stars to entertain the fleet; tattoo studios knew when to top up their ink bottles and sharpen their needles; and the American community knew when their friends in the US Navy would be in town. If they were inexperienced enough to ring up the American Consulate to ask when a friend's ship would arrive in Hong Kong, they were told that the information was 'Top Secret'. Ironically, all they had to do was take a tram down to Wanchai and there, written below the words 'Welcome to all US Servicemen' on placards outside the bars, were lists of all the American warships expected in port for the next two weeks, together with the dates of their arrival. They were said to be ninety per cent accurate. Western intelligence agents were also supposed to be operating in Wanchai, but the image of a CIA or MI6 spy uncovering some dark plot over a glass of green slime seems rather ridiculous today. But silly things happen in troubled times.

The most famous 'spook' in Wanchai was the ghost of the East Town Cinema. If an American sailor took a bargirl there, it was advisable for him to select a lady with a strong bladder: the ghost haunted the ladies' lavatory and no Chinese girl would go near the place. It was said that if you looked in the mirror, the spectre of a wild and distressed woman would appear behind you. If you saw this wraith, you would be struck dead INSTANTLY! How anyone ever lived to tell the tale has never been satisfactorily explained. The cinema was pulled down years ago, but the legend lingers on in an albeit slightly different form: the ghost which is now said to haunt the ladies' powder room of Rigoletto's Italian Restaurant in the East Town Building seems to have changed sex and manifests itself in the shape of a singing hunchback.

It was not only the bars that prospered from the Vietnam War—tailors, restaurants, camera shops, hi-fi emporiums and tattoo parlours all made a killing. The Pinky Tattoo Studio in Jaffe Road was an institution. At times the Blue Sky seemed more like a convalescent home than a bar, as freshly-tattooed sailors staggered through the door with layers of tissue paper taped to them like bandages. After a couple of hours' drinking came the unveiling ceremony and the tissue paper was carefully removed to reveal either the sacred or the profane: The Four Horsemen of the Apocalypse or a voluptuous naked lady, in one case pushing a lawnmower, and all in glorious techni-colour. Pinky emigrated to America a few years ago, but the Ricky and Pinky Tattoo Studio still flourishes under new management.

THE END OF AN ERA

With the end of the Vietnam War, the sailors and the ships departed. Topless bars began to open and the prices went up as the clientele changed to the plastic money brigade—your local wealthy *gweilo*, Chinese or Japanese businessman with a bottomless expense account. Sailors were no longer welcome. The gaudy mini-cheong sams were replaced by equally gaudy evening dresses and dazzling skin-tight disco pants in violent electric blues and screaming pinks. Even the locals were now expected to buy girlie drinks.

Like the plagues of Egypt, disaster soon followed disaster: first there was the great anti-corruption campaign, then the puritanical anti-vice clean-up. By 1980 all that was left were about thirty half-empty bars, struggling to make ends meet. With every calamity the prices went up. New clubs like the Volvo opened up in Tsim Sha Tsui—and the World of Suzie Wong was ready to die. The last straw was the arrival of AIDS. Suddenly, even the most enthusiastic of voluptuaries stayed away.

In recent years there has been a mini-revival, spearheaded by imported Filipina disco dancers. There are still a few aged bargirls left over from the Suzie Wong Era. They sit like wallflowers behind the bar in rose pink and baby blue evening dresses that don't quite fit, waiting for some drunk with an Oedipus complex to walk in and buy them a drink. Bitter, envious and unloved, they place themselves directly between the customer and a gorgeous Filipina disco dancer in a skimpy aerobic costume, gyrating lasciviously on the stage, deliberately blocking the view.

Twenty years ago they would have aggressively demanded a drink, but nowadays, although they still try out of habit, they don't really expect anyone to buy them one. Like Chloe, Flavia and Delia in Alexander Pope's epigram *On Certain Ladies*, Suzie, Tina and Winnie have not yet quite realized that the party is over. Pope wrote:

> 'These ghosts of beauty wandering here reside,
> And haunt the places where their honour died.'

MODERN WANCHAI

It was probably harder for Wanchai to recover from the Suzie Wong Era than from World War Two. The transformation of Wanchai from a sleazy bar area to the vibrant commercial and residential community it is today has been a gradual process. The four most critical events were the sale of the extensive naval and military lands that served as a blockade between Central and the whole of eastern Hong Kong; the building of the Mass Transit Railway; the redivision of Hong Kong Island into four large districts; and the opening of the Hong Kong Convention and Exhibition Centre.

THE SALE OF THE NAVAL YARD

In 1959 the War Department finally agreed to give up most of the Naval and Army land between Murray Road and the Police Headquarters at Arsenal Street, thus 'eliminating the stranglehold round our waist.'

The Financial Secretary A.G. Clarke said, 'At one stage the differences between us were so wide that negotiations were suspended.' However, a compromise was reached at last. The *South China Morning Post* of 8 October 1959 reported: 'Government has agreed to pay £7,000,000 (HK$112 million) for the Royal Naval Dockyard and the Kowloon Yard.' It added that: 'It has also negotiated successfully for the site of HMS Tamar and will credit the War Department with $24 million for this land.'

The Hong Kong Dockyard was 962,000 square feet and the Kowloon site 680,000 square feet. It was not a bad bargain at $68 per square foot. Ten years later, Hong Kong Land paid $4,868 per square foot for the site of Jardine House in Central, which was considered a bargain at the time.

Mr Clarke said it had not been decided what the government would do with the land when it took possession.

In the end they sold most of it at a vast profit. The area is now called Admiralty after its maritime past.

Building Harcourt Road, named after Rear-Admiral Cecil Harcourt, who liberated Hong Kong from the Japanese, did not immediately solve the problem and a whole new infrastructure of roads and flyovers had to be built. It was not until the construction of the final stage of the Island Eastern Corridor, in 1986, that the problem was really solved.

THE MASS TRANSIT RAILWAY

The construction on the Mass Transit Railway (MTR) began in 1975, but the Modified Initial System did not include Wanchai. The nearest station, when it opened in 1980, was Admiralty. However, that year it was decided to go ahead with the Island Line and, in May 1985, the first trains between Central and Wanchai were operating. The Island Line cost $11 billion to build.

During the construction Hennessy Road was dug up and the traffic jams were so appalling that it was often quicker to walk to Wanchai from Central than take a taxi. Once the MTR opened everything changed. Office space in Central District had become too expensive and Wanchai was an attractive alternative. However, the stigma of the Suzie Wong Era lingered on. A few eyebrows were raised if Wanchai appeared on your letterhead, but Hong Kong's real estate magnates can never resist a bargain and soon whole blocks of dilapidated four storey shops were being bought up and demolished and a great new commercial centre began to emerge.

The building had already begun long before the MTR opened. The Arsenal Street end of Lockhart Road was dominated by Asian House, which dwarfed most of the other buildings in the area. In Causeway Bay, there were a number of large department stores like Daimaru and China Products. However, it was the arrival of the Excelsior Hotel and the forty-two storey World Trade Centre in 1975 that was the critical factor in the development. This complex was built by Hong Kong Land on the site of the old Jardine godowns at East Point.

Land Reclamation

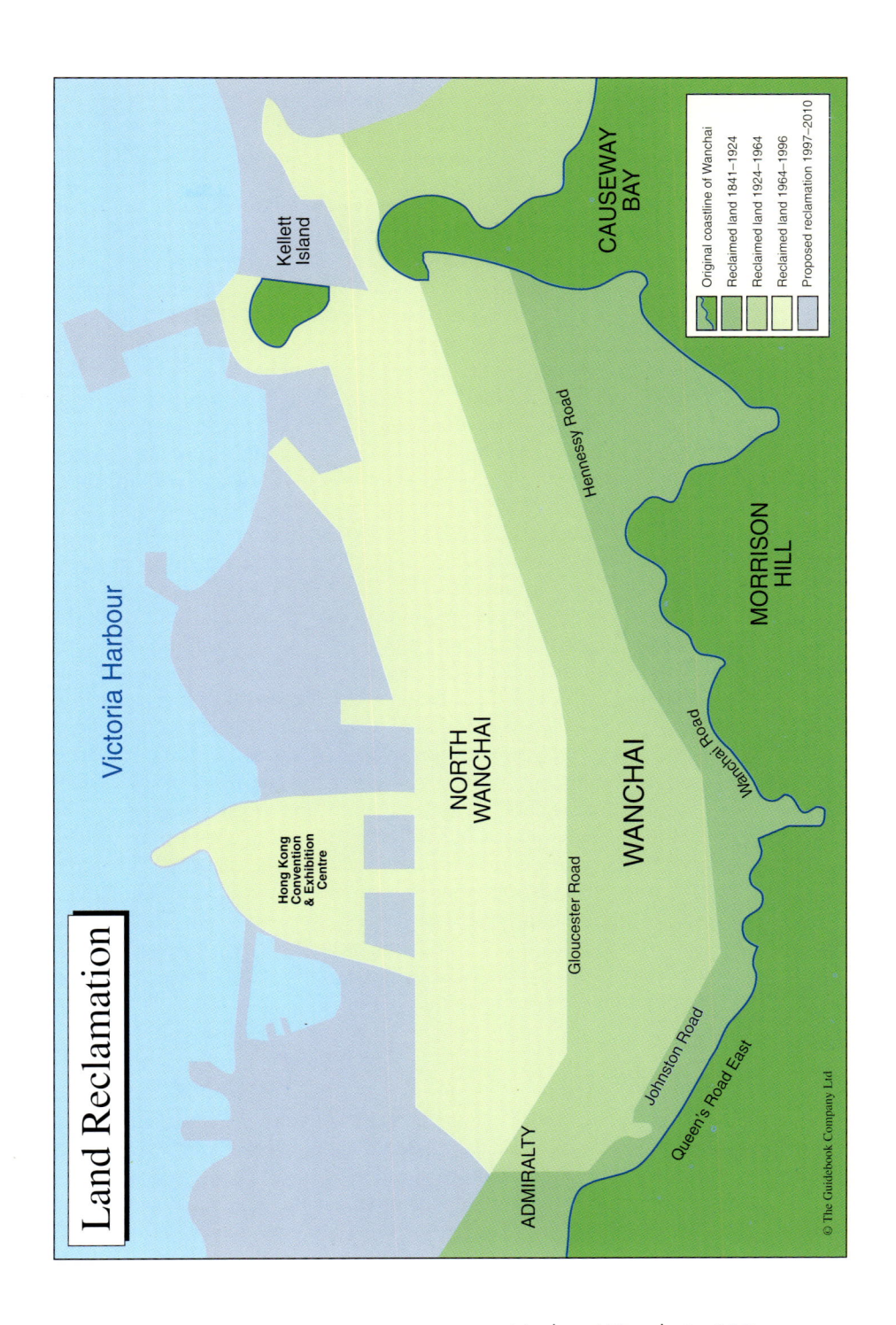

Modern Wanchai 113

The World Trade Centre was originally conceived as an exhibition and convention centre. It hosted the Commonwealth Finance Minister's Conference in 1976, but it was ahead of its time and didn't pay its way. It later became a restaurant and then a cinema. There was also a night club that featured the Bluebell Girls. Before that time exhibitions were generally held in temporary structures on Wanchai Reclamation. For many years the Chinese Manufacturer's Association (CMA) put on an annual exhibition there. It was a cross between a sophisticated trade fair and a flea market. 'Export only' goods were on display and sold at ludicrously low prices, anything from a shirt at two dollars to an electric light bulb for a few cents. There were cooked food stalls and kiosks selling candy floss stood next to stalls displaying the latest thing in high-tech stereo equipment. The CMA Exhibitions were always dominated by the Tiger Balm plywood pagoda. One year the Urban Council had a Lap Sap Chung Aunt Sally. Lap Sap Chung was the anti-hero of the Clean Hong Kong Campaign, a vile red and green spotted litterbug. The game was to throw a tennis ball at a model of him. If you hit the creature in the eye, a bell rang and you were given a plastic Lap Sap Chung Badge as a prize. If you missed you got a Clean Hong Kong sticker. Unfortunately all the balls, which had been donated by the Hong Kong Cricket Club, were stolen on the opening day. There was plenty of exotic Chinese food, the like of which is seldom seen in Hong Kong, such as tinned Chop Suey and Chocolate Ants, manufactured strictly for the export market. The carnival went on for a month and one year over two million people visited it. As it was held in December, it was ideal for doing your Christmas shopping.

WANCHAI DISTRICT

One spring morning in May 1968, the wealthy residents of Jardine's Lookout in their palatial villas and Government Servants in their comfortable quarters on Mount Nicholson woke up to discover, to their astonishment, that they were now living in Wanchai. The Hong Kong Government had decided to divide Hong Kong Island into four large districts. At the turn of the century, District No 8 Wanchai was squeezed between Ha Wan and Bowrington. After the 1920s reclamation, its borders were extended to engulf these two districts. To the south there was Happy Valley, which was a separate district on its own.

Suddenly everything had changed. Under the new scheme, each district had a District Officer. The duties of the District Officer, according to the Hong Kong Yearbook, is to: 'exercise a local co-ordination function, explain policies, test public opinion, watch for sources of grievance and tension, and in general try to soften the impact on the man on the street of the measures adopted by a specialized and sophisticated administration. They also deal with individual complaints, answer enquiries, provide information and mediate in a variety of disputes.'

In 1982 Wanchai District Board was set up as a local advisory and consultative body. Its job is to consider 'not only local matters, but also territory-wide issues which may affect Wan Chai as a whole, such as traffic and transport, public housing, education, medical and health, political and environmental matters, etc.'

The success of the scheme largely depended on the personality and drive of the District Officer and the industry and dedication of the members of the board. Here Wanchai has been fortunate. For six years Wanchai was lucky enough to have as District Officer the dynamic Peter Mann and as chairman of the board the indomitable Peggy Lam, the pioneer of family planning in Hong Kong.

The new border of Wanchai District runs from the old HMS *Tamar* up to Magazine Gap and on to Upper Aberdeen Reservoir. There it turns east to Wong Nai Chung Gap, including what is now the Hong Kong Cricket Club. The boundary then runs north to Jardine's Lookout before turning east to Siu Ma Shan. In a series of steps it goes west again until it reaches the harbour at Causeway Bay. Wanchai's 'new territories' include Mount Cameron, Mount Nicholson, Jardine's Lookout, Tai Hang, So Kon Po, most of Causeway Bay and Happy Valley. At a stroke of the governor's pen, Wanchai had gained a half dozen cemeteries, a pagan shrine, two cricket clubs, a complex of swimming pools, a few sports stadiums, three pagodas and

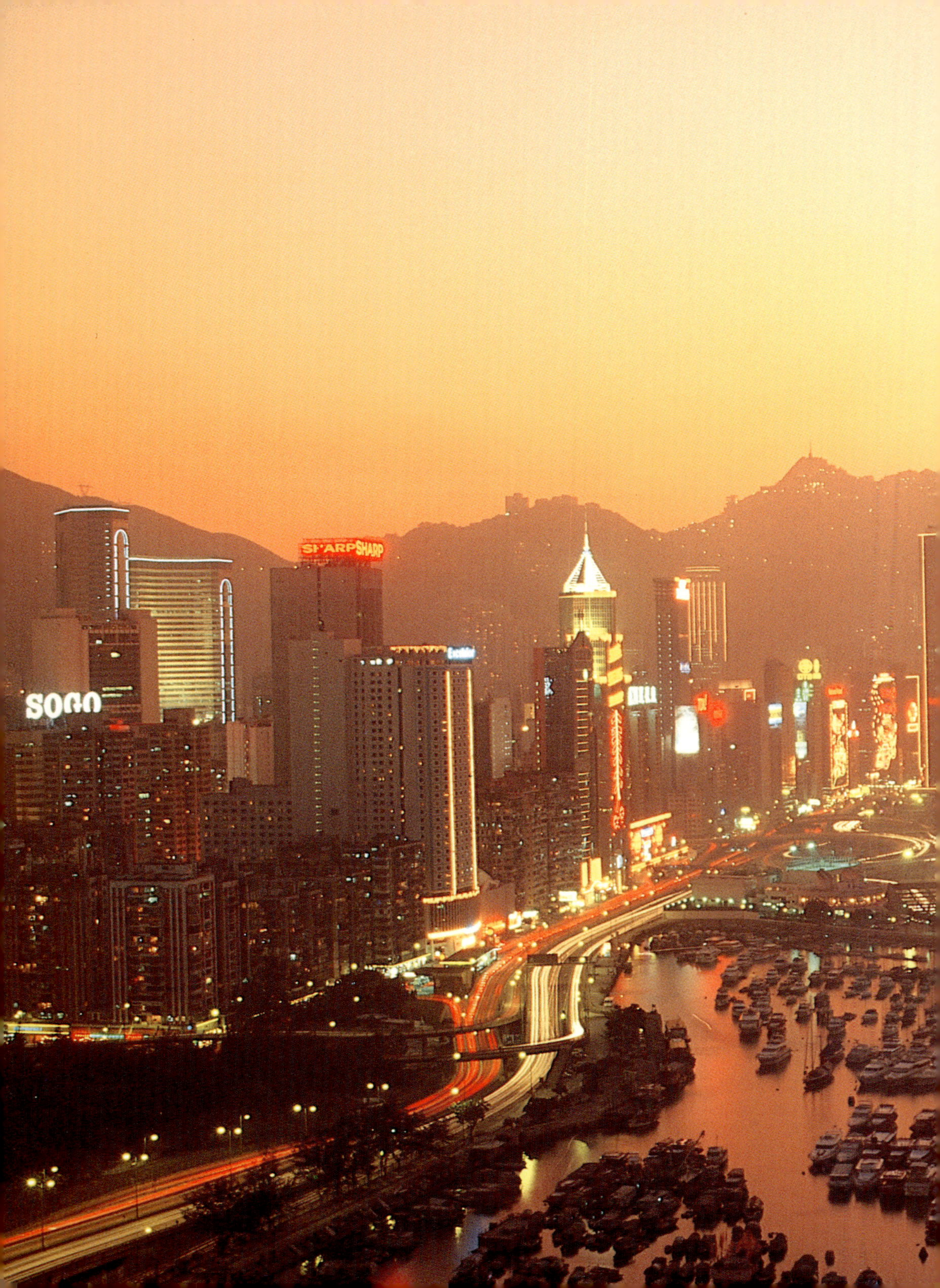
SOGO
SHARP SHARP

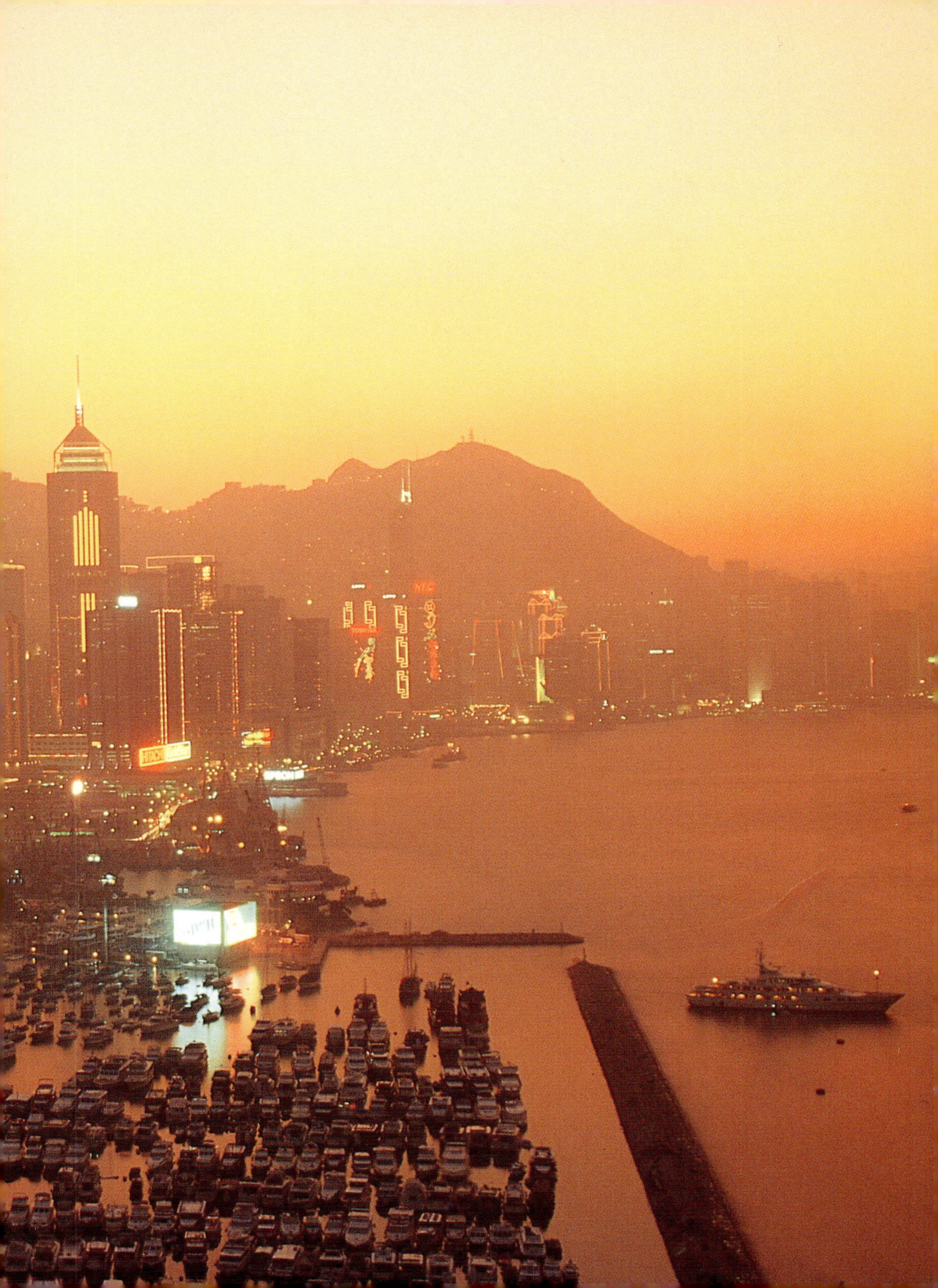

(previous pages) Causeway Bay Typhoon Shelter showing Wanchai in the middle distance.

a race course. Overnight, Wanchai became the sports centre of Hong Kong and, among other things, the venue of the Hong Kong Rugby Sevens. Once a year, the world's finest rugby players put on a brilliant exhibition of mud wrestling before an enthusiastic crowd of thousands. The whole event is beamed around the world on television. The 'Sevens Weekend' is an unofficial expatriate reunion, when old Hong Kong hands, living abroad, return to the Colony to watch rugby, before descending on Lockhart Road for a couple of cold beers with their friends.

HAPPY VALLEY

Although Happy Valley cannot boast of being the place where Hong Kong's first horse race was run—that honour goes to Pok Fu Lam—it came in a close second. Racing started at Happy Valley in 1846, when Hong Kong was a barren rock with hardly a horse upon it. The first races were a shambles. The horses, like their owners and jockeys, were multinational. Australian Walers ran against pure bred Arabs and there were wild China ponies from the steppes of Mongolia. There were army cavalry horses and there were old hacks. There was even a fifty yards race where a man ran against a horse. The man won by a short head; maybe the horse got off to a bad start, anything can happen in racing. The first forty years of racing in Hong Kong were chaos.

In 1884 the top racing men in Hong Kong had had enough. They got together and founded the Hong Kong Jockey Club. The first Chairman was Phineas Ryrie, an all round sporting man. As well as horse racing, Ryrie was fond of shooting. He introduced rabbits to Stonecutters Island for the purpose of rabbit shooting. Unfortunately the rabbits failed to breed like rabbits and the project ended in disaster. There was a snake farm on the island and there was speculation that the snakes ate the rabbits, but it was probably the stonecutters.

It was the second Chairman, Sir Paul Chater, who put racing on a proper footing. He held the post from 1892 until his death in 1926. Chater was descended from a clan of Armenian merchant princes. He founded Hong Kong Land and Chater Garden in Central is named after him.

Going to the races was much more fun in the last century than it is today. Races were held only once a year, during the Chinese New Year holidays, and Happy Valley became a fairground. The other great racing clubs of China, Shanghai and Peking, sent down horses and jockeys by steamer to compete with Hong Kong's finest. The annual race meeting was like one big party that went on for three days—like all parties it had to end sometime.

It happened on a beautiful sunny day in February 1918. To the roar of the crowd, Sir Ellis Kadoorie's *Tytam Chief* galloped home to win the Hong Kong Derby. Sir Ellis and the members of the Hong Kong Jockey Club watched from a luxurious, ornate Victorian grandstand. Non-members either lined the railings of the race track or sat in temporary matshed stands that had been especially constructed for the event.

Just before the China Stakes were due to start, one of the three storey, rickety matshed grandstands collapsed like a house of cards, sending 3,000 spectators tumbling to the ground. Underneath the stand were a number of cooked food stalls, selling tea and *dim sum*. These primitive field kitchens were crushed during the collapse, littering the ground with burning coals. The broken bamboo matting burst instantly into flames and soon the whole grandstand was ablaze.

The ghastly, struggling mass of panic-stricken spectators clawed and trampled over each other as they fought to escape from the relentless flames. Those who were not crushed or trampled to death in the blind panic were roasted alive by the raging inferno. The sickly smell of roasting flesh lingered over Happy Valley for days.

No one knows for certain how many people perished in the holocaust. The official estimate was six hundred dead and four hundred injured. Almost all the victims of the catastrophe were Chinese. A Commission of Inquiry was set up to find out the cause of the accident. As similar matshed grandstands had been around for years without collapsing and there were no guidelines in the Buildings Ordinance on matshed construction, it proved to be a difficult task. Fortunately, it was discovered that the accident took place on Crown Land so the Commission was able to use the poor old Public Works Department as a

March 10th 1918

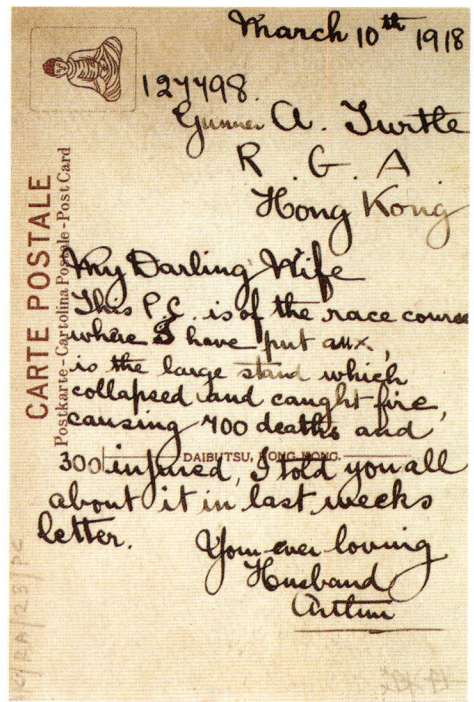

124498.
Gunner A. Turtle
R.G.A
Hong Kong

My Darling Wife
This P.C. is of the race course where I have put aux, is the large stand which collapsed and caught fire, causing 700 deaths and 300 injured, I told you all about it in last weeks letter. Your ever loving Husband
Arthur

120 Wanchai

The Happy Valley Racecourse fire, February 1918.

Gunner Arthur Turtle sent this postcard to his wife, marking the stand where the fire started with a cross.

Modern Wanchai

scapegoat. There is a grim memorial to the victims, decorated with two pagodas, on the hill above Government Stadium.

Today the Hong Kong Jockey Club is one of Hong Kong's great charitable institutions and Wanchai has benefited enormously from its generosity. The magnificent new Hong Kong Stadium was built by the club in 1993, at a cost of $850 million, and the club paid for the Hong Kong Academy for the Performing Arts.

TIGER BALM GARDENS

James Zee-Min Lee described the White Pagoda in Tiger Balm Gardens as 'the one and only outstanding Chinese architectural monument in the entire colony.' Mr Lee was something of an expert on pagodas. He tells us that although China is sometimes called the 'Land of the Pagodas', they are not Chinese at all:

'Originally brought to China from India during the Han Dynasty AD 67, when Buddhism was introduced, the pagoda or poutkhoda, derived from Hindustani, meaning 'Holy House of Gods' was used as a sanctorium in the monastery where Buddhist images and sacred relics were enshrined.'

Viewed on its own, the White Pagoda is a beautifully proportioned building. Unfortunately it is not on its own; it stands in the heart of Tiger Balm Gardens, known locally as 'Hong Kong's answer to Disneyland'. David Perkins, commenting on this observation, wrote: 'Whether you regard this as the ultimate accolade or the final insult depends largely on your nationality; but it does have a ring of truth about it. Had Disney been commissioned to capture the folklore of China in the three-dimensions of concrete, the result might have been the same.'

The Tiger Balm Gardens were built by the Aw family from profits derived from Tiger Balm, a Chinese embrocation made by the Haw Par brothers. Tiger Balm Gardens cost $16 million when it was built in 1935, which gives some indication about the popularity of Tiger Balm. The gardens themselves are full of hundreds of statues depicting Chinese folklore, painted in rather gaudy colours. The Chinese may not have invented the pagoda, but Tiger Balm Gardens is proof in living concrete that they were among the early pioneers of Pop Art, thus dismissing that old canard that Hong Kong is a cultural desert.

JARDINE'S LOOKOUT

The legend of Jardine's Lookout is that Dr William Jardine, founder of Jardine, Matheson & Co, used to sit on the top of the hill with his telescope, watching the clippers approaching the Lei Mun Pass. As soon as he spotted the ship he was looking for, he would send out a fast boat to intercept it and collect the mail. There was no telegraph at that time and this gave him a few hours advance information on what was happening in the rest of the world. The commercial value of this information was immense. This story is, of course, a myth, because Dr Jardine left China in 1839, before Hong Kong became a colony, and never set foot on the island. However, there is a ring of truth in the legend.

Paul King, who was at one time Commissioner of Customs in China, was a great friend of Captain Martin, the skipper of Jardine's paddle steamer SS *Glengyle*. She was built on 'yacht-like lines' and extremely fast. He wrote: 'The *Glengyle* was a vessel with a history. In the old opium days at Hong-Kong she left Calcutta a day *after* the Indian Mail and arrived in Hong-Kong a day or so before her and remained in hiding near Lye-Moon Pass. Her first mate - disguised as a Chinese - landed alone, and delivered the mail advices to the firm that owned her. When the Indian Mail had arrived and the letters were delivered in the usual way, the *Glengyle* also came into port and duly registered her arrival. Meanwhile the "Beati-possidentes" of the latest news had been able to anticipate, "intelligently anticipate", market conditions, very much to their own benefit.' He added, 'But the installation of telegraphic communication spoilt her little game, and she sank to the level of coast boat.'

Jardine's sold the *Glengyle* to John Swire in 1868 and she was the first ship owned by the China Navigation Co. Captain Martin was not aboard her when she struck the Three Chimney Bluff in broad daylight and sank shortly afterwards in deep water. Her temporary captain locked himself in his stateroom and went down with the ship. The Chief Engineer was saved by a Chinese fireman, but there was considerable loss of life.

'Regrets for her loss were more sentimental than real,' wrote King, 'as she was an expensive boat to run for her small size as a carrier. Still her anchor chains and deck fittings were a sight fit for the gods, and no wonder her loss nearly broke Captain Martin's heart. Peace be to her bones 'neath the China Sea!'

WONG NAI CHUNG

Happy Valley has been known over the years by a number of names: Wong Nai Chung Valley, Pau Ma Tei and Belcher Valley. In the 1880s Sir George Bowen, Governor of Hong Kong, bullied the Legislative Council into officially changing its name to Bowen Park, after himself. Bowen was unpopular both in Hong Kong and Britain and was once described as a 'pompous donkey' by Lord Granville, the British Colonial Secretary of that era. He was succeeded as governor by Sir William Des Voeux, whose opinion of Bowen was somewhat similar to that of Lord Granville and was probably responsible for changing the name back to Happy Valley.

In Wong Nai Chung Valley there was a delightful little Chinese village of that name. It was located roughly where Village Road is today. John Thomson, Hong Kong's first great photographer, took three pictures of the valley for *The China Magazine* in 1868. He also wrote an accompanying article. He described the valley 'as full of charms, glimpses of rich scenery, shady woodland, pleasant meadow, lofty hill-land, brooks streams, waterfalls as any spot of the same size which it has ever been my lot to see'.

He set up his camera on the top of Morrison Hill. Looking through a wide angle lens, he described what he saw: 'You can count every post in the Race Course railing. There was a ghastly distinctness about it all.' He didn't bother to take that picture. If photography is an art form, then Thomson was an artist. If he disliked a view, he was reluctant to photograph it. Sometimes he had to. He was not impressed by the Great Wall of China, which he dismissed casually as 'a useless stone fence', but he felt obliged to photograph it. The result was not one of his best pictures.

He explains in his article the reasons why he selected the three particular scenes that were reproduced in the magazine.

John Thomson's 1868 photograph of Wong Nai Chung Village.

'Then there is the village; look how it *nestles*!' he wrote about his picture of Wong Nai Chung Village. His second photograph, which he called a 'lazy peace picture', is not so successful. His third picture of Wong Nai Chung Gap was 'a photograph of a piece of engineering' that destroyed the *fung shui* of the valley, which the Chinese claimed was shaped like a dragon:

'Now in the present case it unfortunately happens that Morrison Hill was the dragon's nose, and when the Gap was made the dragon's nose was cut off from his face. This has made the dragon irate and he intends, we are informed, to hurl dire misfortunes upon Hong Kong one of these fine days.'

The man responsible for cutting off the nose of the dragon was the ill-starred William Tarrant, the vitriolic editor of the *Friend of China*, who had previously worked in the Surveyor-General's Department as the Lands and Roads Inspector. Destroying the *fung shui* of the valley didn't do much good for Tarrant, who spent rather a lot of time in prison and died, a broken man, in Shanghai in 1872.

Thomson also wrote a religious poem about the scenery of Wong Nai Chung as it passed gently through the four seasons of the year. Describing the valley in springtime, he wrote:

> '*Thy beauty walks, thy tenderness and love.*
> *Wide flush the fields; the softening air is balm;*
> *Echo the mountains round; the forests smile*
> *And every sense and every heart is Joy.*'

There are not many sacred poems about the District of Wanchai; most of them tend to be profane. Larry Allen's 'The Wanchai Bargirls' Song' is probably the best known. It begins:

> '*Me no likee Blitish sailor,*
> *Yankee sailor I adore,*
> *Me no likee Blitish sailor,*
> *Yankee pay one dollar more.*'

Returning to things sacred, nothing is more sacred to an Englishman than the noble game of cricket. The Hong Kong Cricket Club moved to Wong Nai Chung Gap in 1975. The leading light behind the founding of the club in Central in 1851, was the corrupt lawyer Dr William Bridges, Tarrant's sworn enemy. At the club's first meeting he proposed a 'democratic committee', with two members representing each of the three social classes: the professional class, the army and tradespeople. Thomas Lane, who founded Lane Crawford, was a member of the original committee. Being a shopkeeper, he presumably represented trade. Dr Bridges said that, although he was happy to play with every 'Tom, Dick or Harry, there was a limit to all things' and he introduced a blackball system. Thomas Lane, whose father had been a humble butler, seems to have been considered respectable. So too was the Armenian Paul Chater, who joined the club when he was a humble clerk with the Bank of Hindustan, China and Japan and played against the Duke of Edinburgh's eleven in 1869.

Above Wong Nai Chung Valley, near Bowen Road, stands a rock which is both sacred and profane. Maiden's Rock is a phallic, rocky protuberance where unmarried girls burn joss sticks and pray for husbands. This granite erectile is also known as Lovers' Rock and is reputed to sometimes answer a maiden's prayer.

THE NORTH WANCHAI RECLAMATION

In 1967, nineteen acres were reclaimed at Wanchai and Causeway Bay for the waterfront road and cross-harbour tunnel. Reclamation had gone on ever since and is unlikely to stop until the whole of the harbour has been filled in, Hong Kong ceases to be an island and North Wanchai becomes South Kowloon or vice versa.

One of the first buildings to be erected on the new reclamation in 1973 was New Mercury House. For four years this eyesore stood on its own on the waterfront, stark and solitary, like a lone loganberry-coloured iced lollypop, dominating the skyline. Thankfully, it is today partially hidden from view by the Hong Kong Arts Centre, which was opened by Governor Sir Murray MacLehose on 10 October 1977. The Arts Centre was entirely funded by public donations from

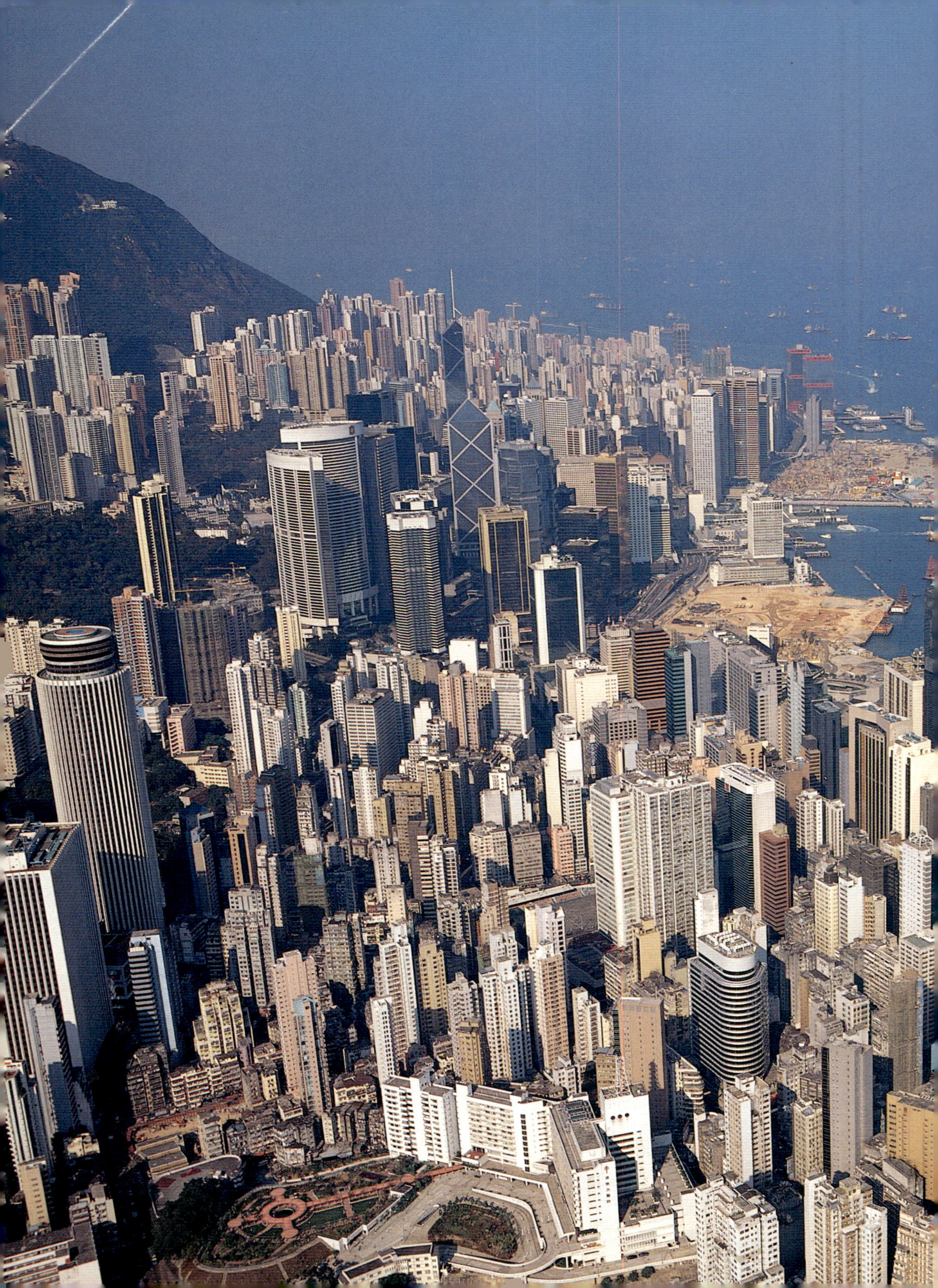

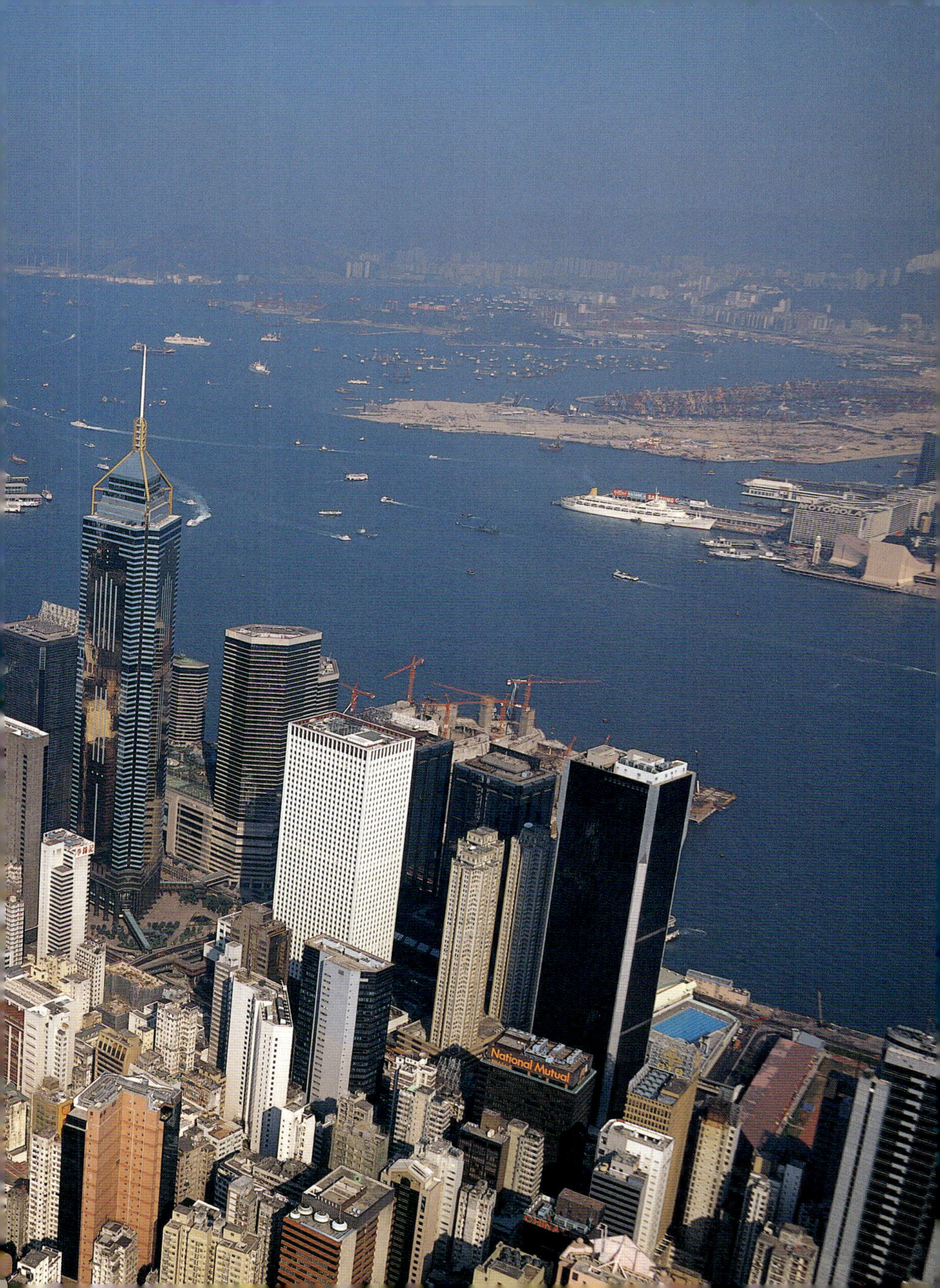
MOTOROLA
National Mutual

(previous pages) 'The Island Reclamation' for the new extension of the Hong Kong Convention and Exhibition Centre is just visible on the right.

individuals and companies. It cost $30 million to build and is nineteen storeys high. During the first year there were just over a thousand separate presentations in its three auditoria, including the debut of the Hong Kong Modern Dance Theatre.

Before the opening of the Pao Siu Loong Gallery in the Arts Centre, local artists complained that Hong Kong didn't have any art galleries, only picture framers. The Arts Centre became a popular venue for the Hong Kong Arts Festival, together with the marvellous old Lee Theatre on Leighton Road, which had a revolving stage, an ornate Baroque interior and was the original cultural centre of Wanchai when it was built by the Lee Hysan family in 1925. The Lee Theatre was also used as a cinema; it was pulled down recently. Although movie buffs may miss the Lee Theatre and the East Town Cinema, with their ghosts, cockroaches and rats, there are now two splendid new cinemas on the reclamation.

North Wanchai, as the reclamation between Gloucester Road and Seafront Road is now known, is an imaginative piece of town planning. As well as the Arts Centre, there is the Hong Kong Academy of Performing Arts, Wanchai Stadium, a training pool and a small park. There are some fine modern buildings. Particularly noticeable is Central Plaza, not only because it is one of the tallest buildings in Asia, but also because it is the finest example of the post-modernist school of architecture in Hong Kong. Post-modernism is both theatrical and kitschy and has its roots in 1920s art deco. It is an ideal style for Hong Kong, because the rules of proportion, which have baffled the territory's architects for so long, are thrown out of the window. Decoration and playfulness replace the austerity of the 'glass box' style of building, which is rapidly becoming unfashionable. A post-modernist Hong Kong is beginning to emerge, with a cityscape of wildly coloured structures, occasionally topped off by the odd playful pagoda roof. The major criticism of Central Plaza is its ridiculous name. It is not in Central—it is in Wanchai.

The choice of name may be in some way connected with the failed conspiracy to emasculate Wanchai by renaming the district Central East, in a snobbish attempt to disassociate the area from a fictitious lady called Suzie Wong. The name Central East, apart from being a bewildering contradiction of terms,

The Hong Kong Rugby Sevens at the new Hong Kong Government Stadium.

It is the people who make a city and Wanchai is one of the most densely populated places in the world. There are hundreds of little businesses whose main customers are local residents and this is one of the great attractions of the place. There are dozens of real street markets that sell everyday Chinese delicacies, anything from dried fish and pressed duck to passion fruit and pomegranates, quite unlike the tourist junk stalls in Central and Stanley, with their Tang Dynasty ash trays, gaudy plastic brocades and fake Rolex watches. When it comes down to value for money, Wanchai is one of the best shopping areas in Hong Kong.

Where food is concerned, Wanchai is superbly cosmopolitan and the selection is fantastic. You can enjoy the cuisine of almost every city and province in China: anything from a humble bowl of noodles at an illegal cooked food stall in a Bowrington gutter, served by an ancient hawker with gold teeth and long hair sprouting out from his moles, clad casually in a dirty vest and boxer shorts, to a sumptuous banquet fit for an emperor, served in a luxurious pleasure palace decorated with golden dragons, where you are waited on hand and foot by lovely Oriental maidens in long, flowing, slinky cheong sams or pampered by plump, obsequious waiters in slick, gamboge dinner jackets, sporting skew-whiff, made-up, maroon bow ties.

Asian food can be found in abundance: Indian, Korean, Mongolian, Thai, Vietnamese, Indonesian, Singaporean, Malaysian, Pakistani; the list is endless. There must be a Tibetan restaurant, but if there isn't, it is no great loss. There are two basic schools of European cooking: the genuine stuff and Wanchai European, which is often absolutely delicious, but seldom quite what one expects. It is important not to be put off by the name of a restaurant. There is, for instance, The Healthy Mess, which serves excellent vegetarian curries, and the ever popular La Bella Donna, which, as every botanist knows, is another name for the poisonous plant deadly nightshade. Some names, like that of the American Restaurant, which serves only Chinese food, are misleading. This one is a throwback from the Vietnam War. There is a restaurant called 369 in Wanchai, which may sound a little suspect if you understand Cantonese number slang. It works something like this: three and six add up to nine and the word for nine is *gau*, which also sounds like the word for dog. As it is illegal to sell dog meat in the Colony, there is, of course, absolutely no suggestion in these pages that any restaurant called 369 actually serves up a dish of man's best friend with its noodles, any more than La Bella Donna laces its spaghetti bolognese with deadly nightshade; but dog lovers should be wary of the odd illegal cooked food stall in darkest Kowloon that has 'Three Six Nine Mutton' on its menu.

French, Italian, German, American, Mexican and even Irish food can be found. Delaney's Irish pub sells two varieties of Irish Stew, one made with mutton for the Catholics, another made with beef for the Protestants. Harry Ramsden's sells Yorkshire fish and chips, as opposed to the Fish and Chips Café, which sells Cantonese fish and chips, and good English pub food can be found in The Old China Hand and The Wanch. There are vegetarian restaurants galore and places which sell vegetarian food. Joe Bananas for instance, recommends its 'Vegetarian Burger with Buffalo Fries', which sounds like the best of both worlds.

WANCHAI: THE ENTERTAINMENT CENTRE

There are still a few girlie bars in Wanchai, but they are very different from those of the Suzie Wong Era. They generally have lively Filipina or Thai disco dancers and can be quite fun, provided you stick to the golden rule of paying for every round of drinks immediately with hard cash. Unfortunately, there are still a few unscrupulous operators around and, after thirty or forty cooling ales, it is quite easy to find oneself presented with a bill for a few thousand dollars for girlie drinks, which you can't remember buying, because you were drunk at the time. During the Vietnam War, seasoned Wanchai Wanderers would only drink beer, because whisky and vodka tended to be manufactured in oil drums in the New Territories, mainly out of menthol alcohol and treacle.

There are now plenty of good old English Pubs, some of which bear a passing resemblance to London pubs and some of which don't. There are upmarket discos, like JJ's in the Grand

Hyatt Hotel, and others like the New Makati, patronized by Filipina amahs looking for husbands and husbands looking for Filipina amahs. There is an abundance of Karaoke lounges. There are yuppie bars, chuppie (Chinese yuppie) bars and sophisticated night clubs where the beautiful people congregate. There are 'Chinese only' bars and Chinese ballrooms, where you can still dance the tango, the waltz and the foxtrot. In the old days, ballrooms were often unlicensed and the only alcohol available was San Miguel, poured surreptitiously from an ancient teapot into a small cup. It is best to go to a ballroom with a Chinese friend who knows the ropes.

Dress code in Wanchai is eccentric and confusing. Only waiters wear dinner jackets. Dress tends to be casual, but not too casual. The China Fleet Club would not allow anyone in wearing flip-flops, but pretty girls in open-toed sandals were never refused entry. This may have something to do with the old adage that 'horses sweat, men perspire and ladies glow'. The China Fleet Club has now closed. There used to be a disco that banned jeans. But as a compromise they provided, for a substantial fee, a rent-a-mini-skirt service. They also went out of business. If you are the proud owner of a mink, don't wear it at Joe Bananas, where the management has an anti-blood sports policy and refuses entry to anyone wearing a fur coat. The bar is named after Joseph Bonanno, a Mafia chieftain, who loved children and dogs and started the Banana War, which left the streets of New York littered with dead bodies in the 1960s; but they were only human beings, which is all right, because *Homo sapiens* is not a protected species.

For music lovers, on Mondays almost every week throughout the year, the Academy of Performing Arts has a free lunchtime recital in its foyer. You have to pay for your food, of course, as there is no such thing as a free lunch. Two or three times a year the Academy puts on a classical opera. They also stage some exciting dance performances, with specially selected vignettes from classical ballet, modern dance, Chinese dance and modern musical theatre, many of which are choreographed by the staff and students of the Academy.

Over the years there have been a series of Wanchai Festivals, Mardi Gras, Carnivals and Food Fairs put on by the Wanchai

Association. In 1992, their magazine announced that the stated aim of one of these events, the Lockhart Road Carnival, was 'to further redress the outdated image of Lockhart Road'. The Wanchai District Officer Peter Mann explained: 'It is not so much a case of whitewashing the area, more of a move towards making Wanchai a cleaner, greener, safer place for all the people of Hong Kong to enjoy.' Included in the programme was a belly dancer.

Writing in the *Wanchai Magazine*, Jackie Abbot described how everybody enjoyed the fun. She wrote: 'Even Mr Stephen Wong, Chairman of the Liquor and Licensing Board, was seen to lean back in his chair while the barman poured copious quantities of tequila and vodka into his mouth and used his head as a mixer.'

This sort of thing would never happen in Central East.

Delivering chicken parts.

WANCHAI 2010

Every great city needs a distinguishing landmark that makes it different from every other great city; Paris has the Eiffel Tower, London has Big Ben and New York has the Statue of Liberty. In some cases the dominant feature of a city is a natural phenomenon, such as the Sugar Loaf Mountain at Rio or the Rock of Gibraltar. Hong Kong is fortunate in this respect, as it has the Peak and still has one of the most beautiful harbours in the world. In the next couple of years it will have two impressive new man-made landmarks, both in Wanchai.

THE MEGA TOWER HOTEL

The aim of the Mega Tower Hotel is to be the tallest building in Asia. Originally it was designed to be sixty storeys high, but the plans were revised and the $3.5 billion project soared to ninety-one storeys, which were later increased by a couple of floors, making a grand total of ninety-three. The agony of creating the tallest building in the world, Asia or Hong Kong, is that sooner or later someone will build a taller one and there is no joy in being second. In Hong Kong, this is more likely to be sooner than later.

The Mega Tower Hotel is the brain-child of Gordon Wu, who is possibly Wanchai's most successful entrepreneur. In an upwardly mobile place like Wanchai, the competition to reach architectural heights is immense. The race for the tallest building in Hong Kong in modern times started with the Connaught Centre, now called Jardine House. This edifice was known as the 'Hong Kong Stilton' because of its porthole-like windows. It was once surfaced with cheese-coloured Welsh slate, but the builders used the wrong adhesive and bits fell off. The structure is now sheathed in tasteful aluminium.

Gordon Wu's Hopewell Centre in Wanchai soon topped

it, followed by Sir Norman Foster's high-tech, off-shore on-shore oil rig, officially known as the Hong Kong and Shanghai Bank. Shortly after the bank was finished, a new Standard Chartered Bank was built next to it, predictably a few feet taller. Then came I.M. Pei's Bank of China Building, which was even bigger. Wanchai's reply was Central Plaza.

Today many of Hong Kong's former tallest buildings have even taller buildings beside, behind and in front of them and, consequently, many of them have almost vanished from sight. In most places, if a building is on the waterfront it is reasonably safe. This is not the case in Hong Kong, with its massive ongoing reclamation. If London were Hong Kong, Big Ben and the Houses of Parliament would probably now be totally obscured by mammoth new office blocks, constructed on land reclaimed from the River Thames.

Where will it all end? Perhaps the answer can be found in the Bible: 'And they said, Go to, let us build a city and a tower, whose top may reach unto heaven; and let us make a name, lest we be scattered upon the face of the whole earth.' Unfortunately, *they* reckoned without divine intervention and God, in his wisdom, put the kibosh on the Tower of Babel. It is highly unlikely that a similar fate awaits the Mega Tower Hotel. The most likely scenario is that, about twenty years after it is finished, it will be demolished and a new and even taller building will be constructed on the site. In Hong Kong, any building over twenty years old is an endangered species and it is soon pulled down to make way for something bigger and better. This is called progress.

AN ISLAND IN THE SUN

Nothing succeeds like success and the popularity of the Hong Kong Convention and Exhibition Centre convinced the Hong Kong Trade Development Council that they needed a larger venue. The most suitable place to build an extension was next to the existing Convention Centre; this meant on reclaimed land.

Unplanned reclamation can be environmentally disastrous, so the planners decided that, in order to stop rubbish piling

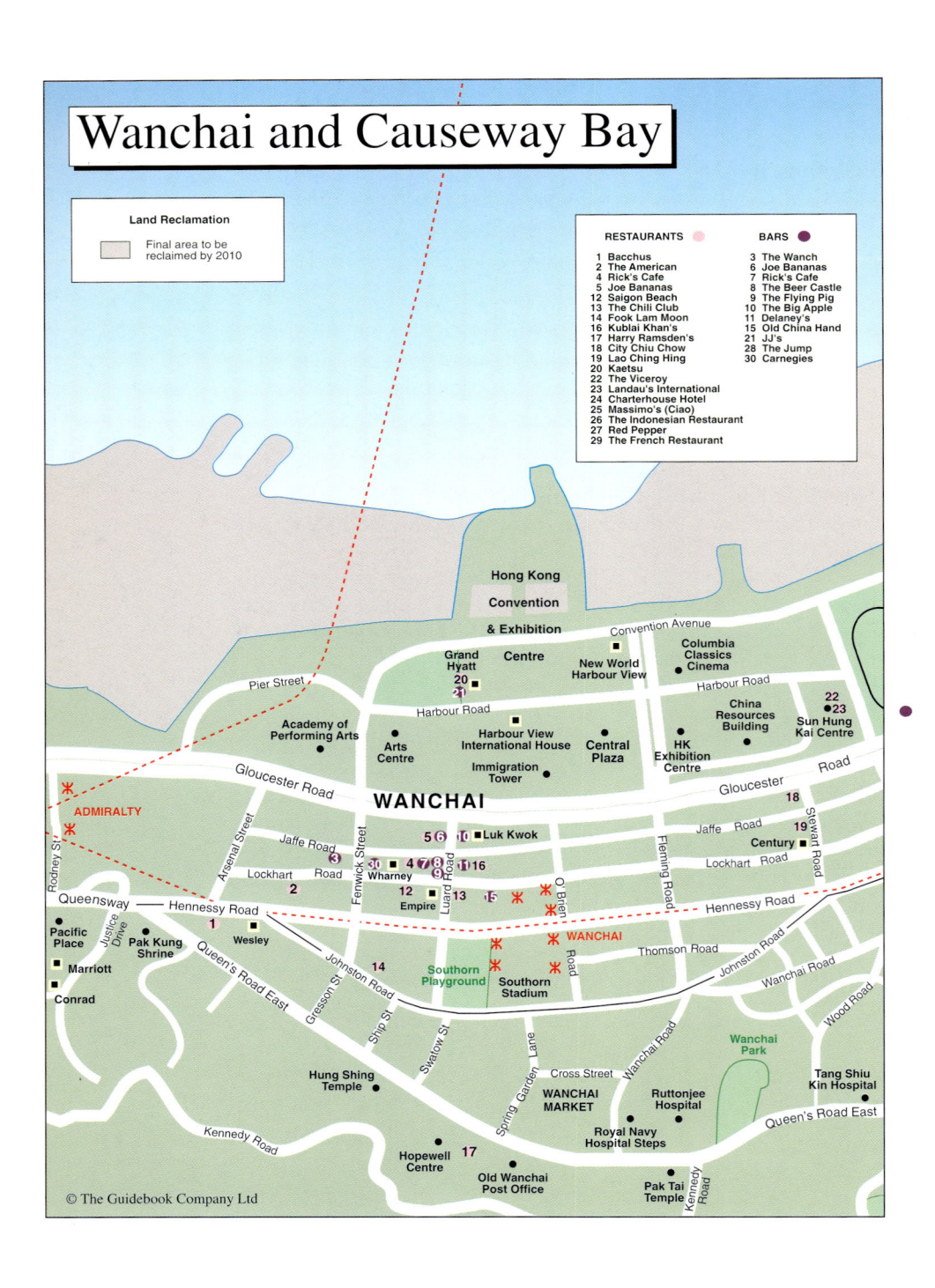

Wanchai and Causeway Bay

Land Reclamation
Final area to be reclaimed by 2010

RESTAURANTS
1 Bacchus
2 The American
4 Rick's Cafe
5 Joe Bananas
12 Saigon Beach
13 The Chili Club
14 Fook Lam Moon
16 Kublai Khan's
17 Harry Ramsden's
18 City Chiu Chow
19 Lao Ching Hing
20 Kaetsu
22 The Viceroy
23 Landau's International
24 Charterhouse Hotel
25 Massimo's (Ciao)
26 The Indonesian Restaurant
27 Red Pepper
29 The French Restaurant

BARS
3 The Wanch
6 Joe Bananas
7 Rick's Cafe
8 The Beer Castle
9 The Flying Pig
10 The Big Apple
11 Delaney's
15 Old China Hand
21 JJ's
28 The Jump
30 Carnegies

Hong Kong Convention & Exhibition Centre
Convention Avenue
Grand Hyatt
New World Harbour View
Columbia Classics Cinema
Pier Street
Harbour Road
China Resources Building
Sun Hung Kai Centre
Academy of Performing Arts
Arts Centre
Harbour View International House
Central Plaza
HK Exhibition Centre
Gloucester Road
Gloucester Road
ADMIRALTY
WANCHAI
Jaffe Road
Luk Kwok
Jaffe Road
Century
Stewart Road
Arsenal Street
Lockhart Road
Wharney
Fleming Road
Lockhart Road
Queensway
Fenwick Street
Empire
Luard Road
O'Brien Road
Hennessy Road
Hennessy Road
Pacific Place
Justice Drive
Wesley
WANCHAI
Marriott
Pak Kung Shrine
Johnston Road
Thomson Road
Johnston Road
Wanchai Road
Conrad
Queen's Road East
Gresson St
Southorn Playground
Southorn Stadium
Wood Road
Ship St
Swatow St
Wanchai Park
Hung Shing Temple
Spring Garden Lane
Cross Street
Ruttonjee Hospital
Tang Shiu Kin Hospital
WANCHAI MARKET
Wanchai Road
Queen's Road East
Kennedy Road
Hopewell Centre
Royal Navy Hospital Steps
Old Wanchai Post Office
Pak Tai Temple
Kennedy Road

© The Guidebook Company Ltd

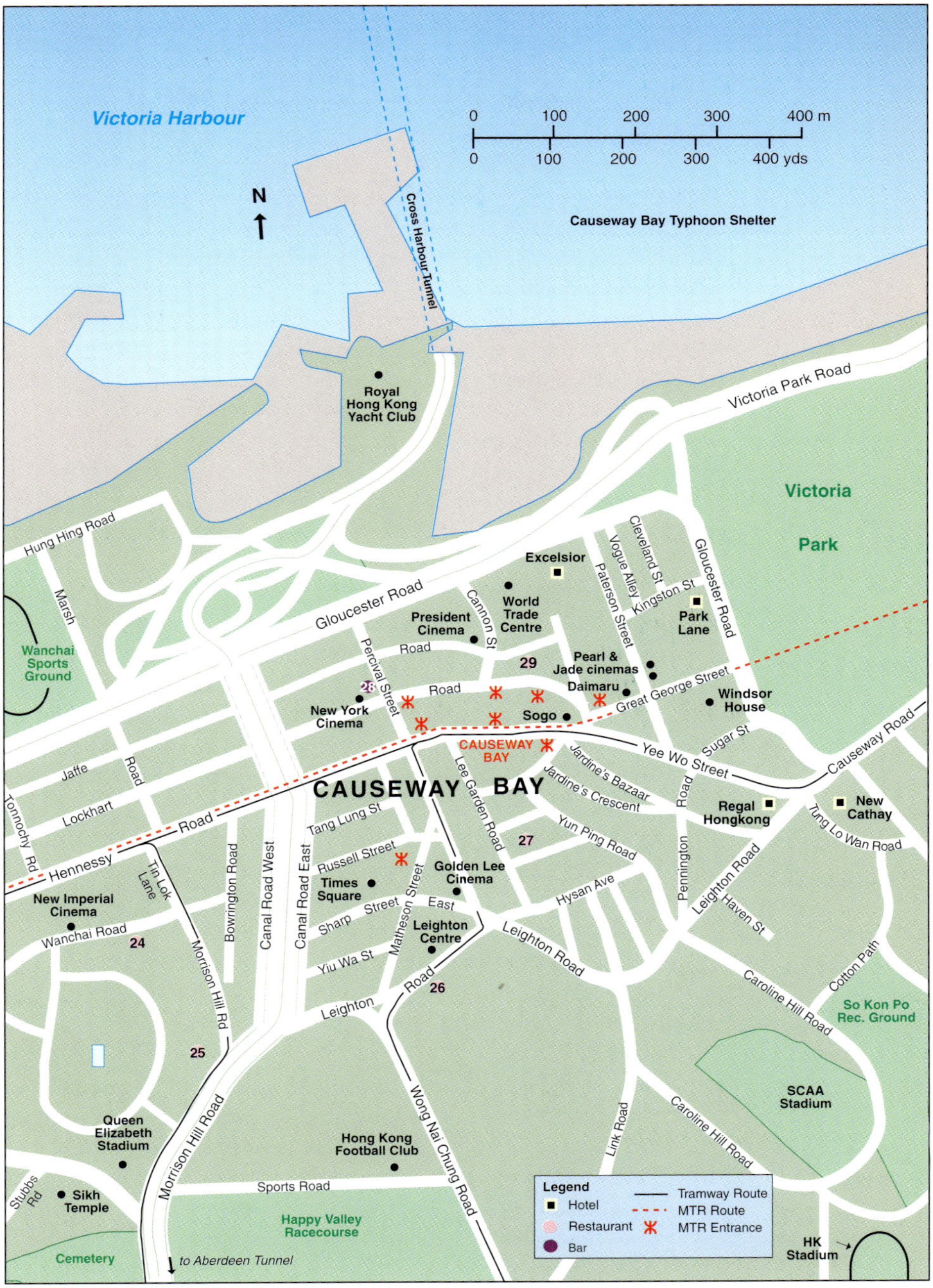
Victoria Harbour
0 100 200 300 400 m
0 100 200 300 400 yds
N
Causeway Bay Typhoon Shelter
Cross Harbour Tunnel
Royal Hong Kong Yacht Club
Victoria Park Road
Victoria Park
Hung Hing Road
Marsh
Wanchai Sports Ground
Gloucester Road
Excelsior
World Trade Centre
President Cinema
Cannon St
Paterson Street
Vogue Alley
Cleveland St
Kingston St
Gloucester Road
Park Lane
Pearl & Jade cinemas
Daimaru
Great George Street
Windsor House
Percival Street
Road
29
28
New York Cinema
Sogo
CAUSEWAY BAY
Yee Wo Street
Sugar St
Causeway Road
Jaffe
Road
Lockhart
Tonnochy Rd
Hennessy
Road
CAUSEWAY BAY
Lee Garden Road
Jardine's Bazaar
Jardine's Crescent
Yun Ping Road
27
Regal Hongkong
New Cathay
Tung Lo Wan Road
Pennington
Leighton Road
Haven St
Tang Lung St
Russell Street
Golden Lee Cinema
Times Square
Hysan Ave
Tin Lok Lane
New Imperial Cinema
Wanchai Road
24
Bowrington Road
Canal Road West
Canal Road East
Sharp Street East
Matheson Street
Leighton Centre
Leighton Road
Yiu Wa St
Morrison Hill Rd
Leighton Road
26
Caroline Hill Road
Cotton Path
So Kon Po Rec. Ground
25
SCAA Stadium
Link Road
Caroline Hill Road
Morrison Hill Road
Queen Elizabeth Stadium
Hong Kong Football Club
Wong Nai Chung Road
Sports Road
Stubbs Rd
Sikh Temple
Happy Valley Racecourse
Cemetery
to Aberdeen Tunnel
Legend
Hotel
Restaurant
Bar
Tramway Route
MTR Route
MTR Entrance
HK Stadium

up on the sea walls and creating a second horrendous Kai Tak Nullah, the new reclamation has been completed in the form of an island in Victoria Harbour, separated from the North Wanchai sea wall by a seventy-five metre water channel, designed to flush away the flotsam and jetsam so prevalent in Hong Kong's fragrant harbour. This project is officially called 'The Island Reclamation'.

The age old problem with reclamation is that new land generally needs a few years to settle before you can build on it. However, with modern technology this is no longer necessary. It is not surprising that this magnificent building with its spectacular flying roof, suberb high-tech modern facilities and one of the most spectacular views of Hong Kong's Fragrant Harbour, was chosen for the historic Handover Ceremony marking the return of Hong Kong's sovereignty to the People's Republic of China.

The reclamation is six and a half hectares, which is roughly equivalent to nine football pitches, and is connected to Wanchai North by two bridges with pedestrian escalators. There will be three large exhibition halls and a business centre, shops, restaurants, car parks, a bus station and eventually it will be connected to the Mass Transit Railway. It will cost almost $5 billion to build and is expected to generate over $30 billion of business a year.

By Hong Kong standards it will be a low rise building and the roof design is shaped to represent 'seabirds soaring into flight over water'. Architects tend to get a bit carried away when describing their masterpieces, but the artist's impression of the project is rather impressive. Comparisons to Sydney Opera House are inevitable, but the extension will be about five times the size and hopefully the acoustics will be better.

Inevitably it will attract more business to Wanchai and that means more offices. Probably the few remaining old buildings in Lockhart and Hennessy Roads will be torn down and replaced by massive new monolithic structures, to cope with the demand for extra office space. Architecturally this will not be a bad thing, as many of Wanchai's early post war buildings have little merit. However, it would be a pity if, as a result, Wanchai's population moved elsewhere and its rich street life vanished, together with the hundreds of charming little bistros, bars, shops and street markets.

WANCHAI 2010

When Bowring launched his Grand Praya Scheme in 1858, he set in motion a programme of reclamation that has never stopped. If you look at the map of Hong Kong as a giant jigsaw puzzle and every fresh reclamation as a new piece of that puzzle, then the 'Island Reclamation' is just the latest piece to drop into place.

There is a second new piece at Blake Pier in Central and in between are the remains of the 'waist', with the old HMS *Tamar* Naval Basin and the Prince of Wales Barracks. The 1994 Sino-British negotiations over the military lands were not the disaster we were led to believe by the local press. Although it was agreed that the People's Liberation Army will retain Prince of Wales Barracks, the important thing is that the Hong Kong Government allowed to fill in the basin and reclaim the land from the harbour which surrounds the barracks. This means that Bowring's original scheme to build a praya from East Point to Sai Ying Pun is at last possible.

There is a superplan to increase the urban areas of the twin cities of Hong Kong and Kowloon by about a third through reclamation. This plan is constantly being changed, refined and updated. It involves not only land reclamation, but roads, railways and tunnels linking urban Hong Kong to the new container ports, airport, Lantau Island and Kowloon. A fantastically complex infrastructure is in the making, of which Wanchai is only a small, but vital, part. In North Wanchai there are still two new pieces of the reclamation jigsaw to drop into place.

The overall plan allows for corridors of open space and the piece of the jigsaw between Blake Pier and the island will be of a distinctly green hue. The whole area will be laid out as an exhibition park, where outdoor displays, concerts and cultural events can be staged. The location of the park is north of the Police Headquarters at Arsenal Street. Across the entrance of the basin will be a bridge, which will link the island to two new ferry piers. There will be a small man-made harbour called the Wanchai Basin. This will not be a yacht marina, but a display area for tall ships, reflecting the Colony's nautical past with tea clippers, windjammers, schooners, lorchas and the odd humble junk on show. Close by will be a maritime museum.

Returning to the Island, there are plans to build a pier with three helipads, jutting out into the harbour to the north of the Convention Centre Extension. This means that, in years to come, helicopters will hover like tiny humming birds somewhere around the beak of the seabird-shaped roof of the building. Eventually, the Island will cease to be an island and the channel will be filled in to make way for a submerged superhighway, which will actually bypass Central. To the east of the Convention Centre will be the bus and MTR stations and two more ferry piers. There will even be a new tramway.

The final piece to the east of the Convention Centre will include the bus and MTR stations and two more ferry piers and offices. This will be the new residential area of North Wanchai. There will be plenty of flats and shops. The present Cargo Handling Basin will be filled in and between the Exhibition Centre and the Royal Hong Kong Yacht Club will be a marina for pleasure craft. A modern Cargo Handling Basin will be incorporated into a new port development scheme at Causeway Bay. Taken all in all, it is a bewildering and breathtaking plan. It is not expected to be completed until 2010.

How will this affect the man in the street? The answer is that in most places the man won't be in the street at all, because a complex upper level walkway and footbridge system will link old Wanchai to the new reclamation and his feet need not touch the ground until he reaches his destination in North Wanchai.

Bowring planned a modest praya, or bund, stretching along the edge of the harbour. The new promenade will be far grander than he could have ever envisaged, with wide, green avenues of trees, gardens, playgrounds and parks, overlooked by thousands of glittering glass towers.

Ariel view of Wanchai and the nearly finished extension of the Hong Kong Convention and Exhibition Centre.

1997 AND ALL THAT

The most frequent question asked of any Hong Kong resident these days is, 'What about the future?' Every Wanchai, Hong Kong or China 'expert' knows that attempting to predict what will happen to Hong Kong after the sovereignty reverts to China is a hazardous business, as there is no known precedent of a third rate economy taking over a first rate economy. Before Mao Tse-tung died, there were hundreds of articles and books published on the fascinating subject of China after Mao. As far as I know, none of the China 'experts' got it right. With this in mind, I formulated 'Hacker's Law'. It is simply this:

> *'Whatever you predict about Hong Kong's future will be wrong.'*

However, there are plenty of theories, ranging from the 'Conspiracy of Optimism' to the Eli Boggs' gloomy 'Doomsday' poem. These have been discussed nightly by Wanchai's intelligentsia for generations, over glasses of cold beer and green slime. Some are worth recording, as they reflect seriously what people think might happen; others are quite bizarre, but they still have a curiosity value:

THE CONSPIRACY OF OPTIMISM THEORY.
That Hong Kong will continue to be a boom town. The Chinese government will not interfere with the running of the Territory and everyone will make a lot of money. This theory took a bit of a bashing after Tiananmen Square.

THE EXPAT 'FULHAM ROAD' THEORY.
That even if the place gets ten per cent worse, or even fifty per cent worse, living in Hong Kong is better than looking at a brick wall in the Fulham Road, Pittsburgh, Dacca or wherever you come from and everybody will make a lot of money.

THE HONG KONG WILL TAKE OVER CHINA THEORY.
China will become so impressed with Hong Kong's success that it will change its laws, its customs, its traditions and its

political system, until it becomes a thriving democracy modelled on Hong Kong and everybody will make a lot of money. This theory is not popular with the present government of China—apart from the money bit.

THE CANTON FACTORY THEORY.
The foreign Factories flourished in Canton successfully for hundreds of years and everybody made a lot of money. Proponents of this theory tend to forget that most of the great East India Companies went bankrupt.

THE FIFTY YEARS THEORY.
That the laws of the Hong Kong Special Administrative Region will not change for fifty years, as laid down in the Sino-British Joint Declaration, therefore Hong Kong's lifestyle will not change for the next fifty years. Carried to its logical conclusion, this means that in 2047 Hong Kong will be fifty years out of date.

THE GRADUAL DISINTEGRATION THEORY.
That after 1997 everything will be fine for a few years, but gradually things will start falling apart and everybody will lose a lot of money.

THE GOOSE THAT LAYS THE GOLDEN EGGS THEORY.
Hong Kong is China's 'Goose that Lays the Golden Eggs' and for this reason its survival is essential to China. Cynics point out that in the original fairy story the goose gets its throat slit.

THE SHANGHAI ENTREPRENEUR TRIBE THEORY.
In its heyday, Shanghai attracted a nucleus of entrepreneurs from all over China. After 1949 they moved to Hong Kong. If things go wrong they will move on to Vancouver, taking Hong Kong's Cantonese entrepreneurs with them.

THE HONG KONG HAS PEAKED THEORY.
This theory has been popular on and off since 1841. Meanwhile, Hong Kong has prospered.

A close up of the spectacular Hong Kong Convention and Exhibition Centre.

148 Wanchai

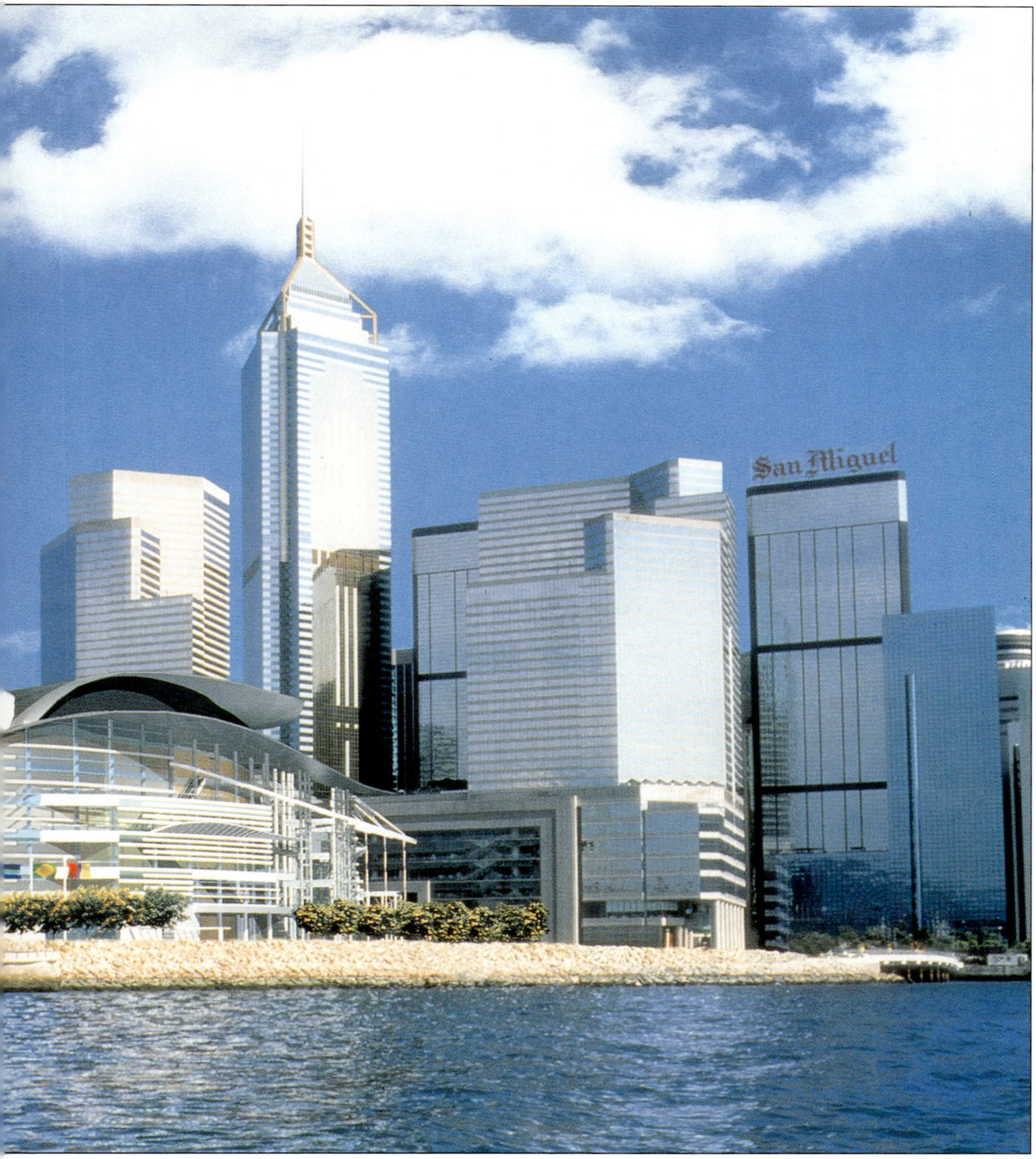
San Miguel

THE ELI BOGGS DOOMSDAY (NOT VERY GOOD POETRY) THEORY.

'Some day p'raps earthquakes her foundation
Will shake to its deep base in the sea.
A blessing 'twill be to each nation
When she's crush'd to all Eternity.'

THE SHARK IN THE SWIMMING POOL THEORY.

Question: If you have a shark in your swimming pool how do you kill it?
Answer: You pull out the plug.
The theory is that if China gets fed up with Hong Kong, somebody will pull out the plug on the Daya Bay Nuclear Power Station.

THE RIVERS OF BLOOD THEORY.

The entire population of Hong Kong will be shot at dawn in the new Government Stadium and their relations in Canada will have to pay the bill for the bullets.

THE OLD CHINA HAND THEORY.

It all depends what happens in China. As nobody has a clue what will happen in China in the next few years, this gets us back to: 'Whatever you predict about Hong Kong's future will be wrong.'

Only one thing is certain and that is that the population of Hong Kong will live in interesting times.

WANCHAI: THE FINALE

In the century and a half following the British arrival in Hong Kong, Wanchai has changed dramatically from an almost unpopulated sandy little bay into a Xanadu of steel and glass towers, marbled halls, pleasure palaces, seabird-shaped business domes and cooked food stalls. Unlike Xanadu, which was created to glorify a 'barbarian' Mongol Emperor, Wanchai is a humble by-product of a 'barbarian' British Empire. Without Kublai Khan and his Mongol hordes, Xanadu would never have existed and without Captain Elliot and nineteenth century British imperialism, who knows what Wanchai would be like today.

'District', 'suburb', 'area' and 'neighbourhood' are totally inadequate words when it comes to describing the Wanch. When a place is unique, there is a tendency to hijack its name. If Stockholm is called the 'Venice of the North' and Bangkok the 'Venice of the East', maybe someday, somewhere, there will be a 'Wanchai of the West', possibly in Vancouver. Wanchai has a powerful international identity and it is a name that conjures up exotic images of a place where the East intermingles with the West in a strange and frantic harmony. The other three districts of Hong Kong Island are characterless by comparison and have dull unimaginative names: Western District, Eastern District and Central District. I like to think that when the districts of Hong Kong Island were renamed in 1968, the Governor of that time, Sir David Trench, who I have been told occasionally dropped into the Wanch for a drink in his youth, had a hand in retaining the name Wanchai. Fortunately, Sir John Bowring's egotistical attempt to change the name to Bowrington failed—although to be fair, Wanchai as we know it today owes a lot to his vision. But Bowrington is not a pretty name and, because he started a totally unnecessary war between Britain and China, it would probably not have survived the post-1997 era anyway. In spite of Wanchai being built almost entirely on reclaimed land, it never suffers the indignity of being called the 'Holland of the East'. Presumably this is because the only tulips to be found in the Wanch are plastic, there are no windmills, the Chinese don't like cheese and anyway Wanchai is a far more exciting place to live in than the Netherlands.

Wanchai is really three entirely different places: the beautifully planned, modern, expensive commercial district of North Wanchai; the semi-rural middle class residential area called Wanchai District; and Old Wanchai with its busy, bustling, cosmopolitan community. Today, the descendants of the Dog of Yao are probably chartered accountants. There are still plenty of pirates, but nowadays they are vendors of plagiarized software, illegal videos and fake designer jeans and their prey are not the great, bat-winged merchant junks with their cargoes of peacocks, opium and silver, but the gullible tourist with his diddy-bag of Deutsche Marks, dollars, credit cards and Japanese yen. There are fewer sailors and consequently fewer bargirls. As for colonialism, that unfashionable word, there are far more former Wanchai residents busy colonizing Canada, Australia and the United States of America than there were ever British colonialists living in Wanchai in the heyday of the British Raj.

As L.P. Hartley said: 'The past is a foreign country: they do things differently there.' Elderly authors, Old China Hands and seafaring men are allowed, from time to time, to wallow in nostalgia, provided that they don't go on for too long. For me, the Wanch is a very special place, littered with happy memories. In Bowrington Street I tasted my first mango. In the Press Club I had my first and last nibble of that great antipodean institution, the Australian meat pie. There was Brandy Nancy's laugh, Alice the Venus-Drink-Trap's vicious left hook and Hitler Lau's remarkable rendering of 'Yummy, Yummy, Yummy—I got luv in my tummy.' I have memories of delicious dinners in the Yaik Sang Restaurant, which had two kinds of fried milk on the menu and somehow you always ended up with the wrong one. There were noodles under the Canal Road flyover in the rain; luscious Crabmeat Pancakes and steaming Spotted Dick in Landau's; flaming Sambucca, spaghetti, garlic and ghost stories in Rigoletto's. The hours spent in Artland selecting coloured papers for the backgrounds of postage stamp designs. Elegant conversations with Spring Water in the Pussycat Bar. Trying to find a computer shop in the Computer Centre. Looking up the correct spelling for Chomondely in the British Council Library and being slung out of the China Fleet Club for wearing flip-flops . . . . and, of course, there was the fictional Suzie Wong. Enough of yesterday.

In the Wanch something is always happening. It is an emporium of pulsating energy. Wanchai is one of the few places in the world where you feel one hundred per cent alive, twenty-four hours a day, today and every day. Like the Windmill, it never closes. Perhaps this is the secret of its success.

A town planner's rendering of the Wanchai of the future.

INDEX

Aberdeen 10
Ahlum Cheong 37, 38–42, *38–39*, 57
Albany Godown 28, 70
Alice the Venus-Drink-Trap 101, 102, 152
Allen, Larry 87, 126
American Restaurant 134
Amoy Street 61
d'Andrâde, Simao 15
Anstey, Thomas Chisholm 40, 41, 46, 52–6
Antiquities Advisory Board 81
Anton Street 64, 68
Arrow War, the 25, 34–36, 49, 55, 65, 66, 88
Arsenal Street 31, 56, 58, 76, 111, 112, 144
Asile des Sainte Enfrance 68
Bain, William 63
Barrett, Ken 89, 97
Bart, Lionel 99
Belcher, Captain Sir Edward 25, 62
Belilios, Emmanuel Rafael 61
Blake, Sir Henry 58
Blenkin Rawson House 28
Blue Buildings 71, *78*
Blue Sky Bar 105–8
Boggs, Eli 44–52, *45*, 146, 150
Bonham, Sir George 29, 33
Bowen, Sir George 124
Bowen Road 127
Bowring, Sir John 33–37, 39, *40*, 41, 42, 44, 52–8, 60, 142, 144, 151
Bowring, Lady 37
Bowrington 44, 56, 115, 134, 151, 152
Bowrington Canal *43*, 56, 68, 76
Bowrington Street 56, 152
Brandy Nancy 105, 152
Bremer, Commodore Sir JJ Gordon 25
Bridges, Dr William Thomas 40–42, 52–54, 56, 127
Broadwood Road 82
Bruce, Murdoch 28, *28–29*
Bruce, Phillip 84, 88
Buckmaster, Admiral 86
Buddington, Captain James 62
Bulwer-Lytton, Sir Edward 53
Burkhardt, V.R. 70

Burn, D.L. 30
Burn MacVicar & Co 30
Burns Pier 30
Caine, Major William 27, 31, *32*, 54, 55, 57
Caldwell, Daniel 40, 45, 48, 49, 52–54, 56
Canal Road 56
Canton 8, 15–19, 22, 30, 33–35, 68, 77, 105, 147
Canton Bazaar 30, 68
Carvalho, Mr. 46
Central Plaza 130, 139
Chan, Andley 73
Chan, Jacqui 99
Chater, Sir Paul 30, 68, 118, 127
Chek Lap Kok 14
Cheng, Mrs. 14, 15, 23
Chiang Kai-shek, Madame 86, 100
China Fleet Club 71, 87, 88, 136, 152
Chinese Methodist Church 81
Chun Tai-kwong 53
Churchill, Winston 73
Clarke, A.G. 111
Clarke, Sergeant 73
Clavell, James 88
Cleverly, Charles St George 55
Clinton, President Bill 63
Cochrane, Admiral Sir Thomas 27
Coe, Peter 99
Collinson, Lieutenant T.B. 26
Colville, Captain 48
Cooke, George Wingrove 45, 52
Coward, Sir Noel 64, 65
Cowper, John 65, 66
Cree, Edward 27
Cromwell, Oliver 28
D'Aguilar, Major-General 31, *32*
Dairy Farm Company 63
Davies, H.T. 55
Davis, Sir John 27, 29, *32*
Day, John 54
Delaney's 135
Demuth, Nick 96
Dent & Co 54
Dent, John 44, 54–56
Derby, Lord 55
Des Voeux, Private Sir Edward 83
Des Voeux Road 42, 54

Des Voeux, Sir William 124
Duddell, George 57
Duncan, John 76
East India Companies 11, 15–19, 147
East Point *12–13*, 25, 26, 31, 42, 44, 60–65, *62*, 72, 112, 142
East Town Cinema 109, 130
Electric Street 30
Elizabeth II, Queen of England 131
Elliot, Captain 22, 23, 25, 72, 151
Emery, Charles 66
Evelyn, John 28
Ever Victorious Army 52
Ewo Shanghai Brewery 77
Excelsior Hotel 31, 112
Esing Bakery *34*, 37, *38*, 39
Factories, the *16–17*, 33, 35, 147
Feng Yu-hsiang, General 80
Fenwick, George 66
Fenwick & Morrison 66
Fenwick Street 66
Fleming, Sir Francis 80
Fleming, Ian 88, 93
Foster, Sir Norman 139
Frazer, George 66
Gahagan, Private G.E. 83
Garden Road 58
George V, King of England 77
Giblin, Mick 85
Gillespie, Charles Van Megan 70
Gloucester, Henry Duke of 77
Gloucester, Richard Duke of 77
Gloucester Road 76, 77 81, 130
Gordon, General Charles 'Chinese' 49
Gough, Sir Hugh 24
Great George Street 63
Great Praya Scheme 42–44, 54, 55, 142
Gresson Street 64, 73–76
Han Suyin 88
Happy Valley 26, 30, 35, 42, 58, 68, 115, 118–122, *120–121*, 124
Harcourt, Rear-Admiral Cecil 86,112
Harcourt Road 112
Harry Ramsden's 135
Hartley, L.P. 152
Hayes, Captain 'Bully' 47–48
Healthy Mess 134
Hennessy, Sir John Pope 78, 80

154 Wanchai

Hennessy Road 76, 81, 112, 140
Hillier, Charles 27
Hing, A. *59*, 68
Holden, William *90–91*, 99
Hong Kong Academy of Performing Arts 122, 130, 136
Hong Kong and Whampoa Docks Company 58, 66
Hong Kong Arts Centre 127, 130
Hong Kong Convention & Exhibition Centre 111, *128–129*, 131, 139–142, 144, *148–149*
Hong Kong Cricket Club 115, 126
Hong Kong Government Stadium 122, *132–133*
Hong Kong Jockey Club 118–122
Hong Kong Trade Development Council 139
Hong Kong Volunteers 82
Hongkong Ice Company 63
Hospital Hill 28
Hughes, Dick 93
Hughes, Lieutenant Colonel H. Owen 82
'Hughesiliers', the 82–83
Hulme, John 27, 31, 39, 41, 46, 55
Hung Shing Temple 67, 69
Ice House Street 54
Innes, James 19, 29
Iquan, Nicholas 11, 14
Isherwood, Christopher 97
Jacosta, Captain 82
Jaffe, Daniel 77
Jaffe Road 77, 80, 105, 109
Jardine's Bazaar 63
Jardine's Lookout 114, 115, 123–124
Jardine, Matheson & Co 25, 26, 31, 60–64, *62*, 72, 77, 82, 112, 123
Jardine, Dr William 19, 29, 123
Jeffery, Captain 31
Jimmy's Kitchen 86–87
JJ's 135
Joe Bananas 135, 136
Johnston, Sir Reginald 80
Johnston Road 71, 76, 80, 81
Jorrock's Hall 70
Kadoorie, Sir Ellis 119
Kam Tin 10, 11
Kao Tsung, Emperor of China 10
Kellett, Sir Henry 61–63

Kellett Island *2–3*, *12–13*, 61–63
Kennedy, President John F. 63
Kennedy Road 58
Keying, Commissioner 27, *32*
King, Paul 123
King's Road 83
Kingston Street 61
Korda, Sir Alexander 89
Koxinga 14
Kuan Yin 70, *71*
Kwan, Nancy *90–91*, 96, 99
Kwong Sang, PC 73
Kyle, John 63
La Bella Donna 134–135
Labouchère, Henry 44
Lam, Peggy 115
Lamont, Captain John 65, 66, 72
Lan Fat 66
Landau, Aaron 87
Landau's 87, 152
Langdale Street 64
Lantau 11, 142
Lapraik, Douglas 65, 66, 72, 73
Larkins, Captain 29
Larkins Pier 29
Lau, Hitler 104, 152
Le Carré, John 88
Lean, David 89
Lee, James Zee-min 122
Lee Theatre 130
Leighton Road 61, 83, 130
Lethbridge, H.J. 73
Levin, Bernard 98
Lewis, Bill 72
Lichfield, Lord 131
Lin, Commissioner 22, 23
Lin Fa Kung Temple 70–71, *71*
Lindley, Augustus F. 49, 52
Lindsay & Co 28, 54
Lindsay, Oliver 83
Lockhart, Sir James Stewart 77
Lockhart Road 78, 87, *103*, 112, 118, 137, 140
Lok Kan School 68
Lover's Rock 26, 127
Luard, Major-General C.C. 80
Luard Road 80, 104, *106*, 107
Luk Kwok Hotel 92, 93, 96
Lun Fat Street 74
Ma Chow Wong 45, 48, 49, 52, 53

Macau 8, 11, 15, 25, 29, 37, 40, 41, 73, 96
Macdonald, Lieutenant 31
Macdonnell, Sir Richard Graves 61
MacDougall & Co 66
MacLehose, Sir Murray 107, 127
Magnificent Ugly 102
Maltby, Major-General C.M. 84
Man, Captain C.M.M. 83–84
Manchu 8, 14, 15, 19, 22–25, 27, 34–36, 80
Mann, Peter 115, 137
Marriott, Mrs. 74
Marriott, Sergeant 'Kid' 74
Marsh, Sir William 80
Martin, Captain 123, 124
Mason, Richard 88–101
Matheson, James 19
Matheson Street 63
Maugham, W. Somerset 88
May, Charles 46, 48
May, Sir Henry 75
McClure, Sir Robert 61
McDonald & Co 66
McGregor's Barracks 70
McGregor's Street 70
McWalter, Sergeant 74
Mega Tower Hotel 138–139
Mercer, William 41, 53, 55
Middlesex Regiment 82–84
Moon Street 30
Morgan, Captain William 25, 60, 68
Morgan's Bazaar 68
Morrison Hill 25, 26, 69, 76, 124, 126
Morrison, J.R. 26
Morrison, Robert 26
Mount Cameron 115
Mount Nicholson 114, 115
Mount Shadwell 26
Mountbatten, Lady 86
Munroe, Matt 87
Murrow, Yorrick 57
Murray Road 58, 111
Nagasaki Joe Hotel 88
Neptune Bar 100, 108
New Mercury House 127
New Territories 10, 82, 135
Ng Choi 80
Noon Day Gun 64
North Point 60, 82
O'Brien Road 84
Ocean Bar 103–104, 108

Index 155

O'Higgins, Bernardo 22
Old China Hand, the 135
Opium 19–23, *20–21*, 29, 30, 45, 52, 53, 152
Opium War, the 23–25, *32*
Oriental Sugar Refinery 61
O'Sullivan, Inspector 73
Our Lady of Mount Carmel Church 68
Pacific Place 30, 84
Pak Kung Shrine 69
Pak Tai Temple *67*, 70
Palmerston, Lord 27, 36, 55
Pan, Major-General H.K. 86
Parkes, Harry 34–36
Paterson, Major J.J. 82
Paterson Street 63
Pei, I.M. 139
Perceval, Alexander 63
Percival Street 56, 63, 76
Perkins, David 122
'Peter the Painter' 73
Pinky Tattoo *94*, 109
Pirates 11–15, 23, 44–53, 151
Plaza Ballroom 87
Pok Fu Lam 73, 118
Pope, Alexander 110
Pottinger, Sir Henry 70
Praya East *2–3*, 68, 71, 76–77
Press Club, the 107, 152
Pu Yi, Emperor of China 80
Pussycat Bar *92*, 101, 102, 104, 108, 152
Quarry Bay 15, 58
Queen's Road *6*, 26, 42, 54, 58, *59*, 68, 69, 70, 72, 74, 77, 81, 82, *82*
Rednaxela Terrace 64
Repulse Bay 26
Rigoletto's 109, 152
Robertson, Major 75
Robinet, W.M. 37
Robinson, Mr. 31
Robinson, Sir Hercules 56–57, 61
Royal Hong Kong Yacht Club 63, 144
Royal Naval Canteen 71, *78*
Royal Naval Dockyard 58, 72, 76, 111
Rugby Sevens 118, *132–133*
Rustomjee, Herjeebhoy 26

Ruttonjee, Jehanghir 27
Ruttonjee Sanatorium 27, 28
Ryrie, Phineas 118
St. Francis Chapel 68
St. Francis Street 30, 68
St. Joseph's Hospital 68
St. Margaret's Church 82
Saltoun, Major-General Lord 64, 72
Sam Pan Street 30
Scandal Point 31
Schooner Street 30
Seafront Road 130
Shadwell, Admiral Charles 26
Shan Kwong Road 82
Ship Street 74
Sikh Temple 82
Silver 18, 19–23, 45, 152
Sim, Inspector 73–74
Singh, PC Mullah 74
Singh, PC Tana 74
So Kai, PC 73
Southorn Playground 80, 86
Southorn, Sir Thomas 80
Spring Gardens 28, 29, *28–29*, 65, 76
Spring Water 104, 152
Star Street 30, 69
Stark, Ray 99–100
Stewart, Sir Frederick 80
Stewart Road 76
Stubbs Road 82
Sun Street 30
Sun Tai, PC 73
Sutherland, Sir Thomas 66
Swatow Street 61
Swire, John 123
Tai Ping Shan 58
Tam Kung Temple 82
Tamar, HMS 115, 142
Tan, A 68
Tang Tzu-ming 10
Tang Wui, PC 74
Tarrant, William 42, 53–55, 57, 126, 127
Tea 18, 19–23
Teng Ting-chen 22
Thomson, Alexander Macdonald 80
Thomson, John 124–126

Thomson, Lord 93
Thomson Road 80
Tiger Balm Gardens 122–123
Tonnochy Ballroom 81
Tonnochy, Malcolm Straun 80
Trench, Sir David 151
Tsai Chin 98, 99
Tsim Sha Tsui 98, 101, 110
Tuen Mun 10, 15
Tung, Mandarin 27
Tung Tsai Tseung Kee & Co 68
Tung Lin Kok Yuen Monastery 82
Turner, Reverend John 60
Tynan, Kenneth 98
Victoria Barracks 58, 60
Victoria Gaol 48, 49, 81
Victoria Harbour 23, *63*, *116–117*, 138, 140
Victoria Hotel 72
Victoria, Queen of England 23, 25, 62
Wanch, the 135, 151
Wanchai Festival 136–137
Wanchai Post Office 70
Wanchai Police Station 73, 81
Wanchai Road 28, *46*, 76, 81
Wanchai Stadium 130
Wang Hung 15
Weddell, John 15
Wei Wong, Emperor of China 11
Weihaiwei 78, 80
Wellington Barracks 58, *59*
Whampoa Mud Docks 65
Whittaker, Dick 72
Williams, Kenneth 87
Wills, Sergeant 75
Wong Nai Chung 115, 124–127, *125*
Wong, Suzie 88–110, *90–91*, 111, 112, 130, 152
World Trade Centre 112, 114
Woolf, Virginia 80
Wong, Stephen 137
Wu, Gordon 138, 139
Yaik Sang 152
Yates, Bob 84, 88
Yee Wo Street 77
Yeh, Ming-chen 33–36, *35*, 57, 65
Yi Wong, Emperor of China 11
Young, Sir Mark 84

BIBLIOGRAPHY

Atwell, Pamela, *British Mandarins and Chinese Reformers*, Oxford University Press, Hong Kong, 1985.

Balfour, S F, *Hong Kong before the British*, The Journal of the Hong Kong Branch of the Royal Asiatic Society, 1971.

Bard, Solomon, *Traders of Hong Kong: Some Foreign Merchant Houses, 1841–1899*, Urban Council, Hong Kong.

Barrett, Ken, *He Knew Suzie*, Hong Kong Tatler Annual, 1989.

Belcher, Captain Sir Edward, *Narrative of a Voyage round the World in Her Majesty's Ship Sulphur*, London, 1843.

Birch, Alan, *Hong Kong: The Colony That Never Was*, Odyssey, Hong Kong, 1991.

Bruce, Phillip, *Second to None*, Oxford University Press, 1991.

Bruce, Phillip, *Hong Kong Military History Notes*, Issue 7, Phillip Bruce, 1987.

Bruce, Phillip, *History Notes*, Issue 1, Ellerbeck Ltd, Hong Kong, 1989.

Burkhardt, V.R., *Chinese Creeds and Customs*, South China Morning Post, 1955.

Chambers, Gillian, *Supertrader*, Hong Kong Trade Development Council, Hong Kong 1989.

Chao, G.H., *The Life and Times of Sir Kai Ho Kai*, The Chinese University Press, Hong Kong, 1981.

Coates, Austin, *China Races*, Oxford University Press, 1983.

Coates, P.D., *The China Consuls*, Oxford University Press, 1988.

Cooke, George Wingrove, *The Times* newspaper, London, 1859.

Collis, Maurice, *Foreign Mud*, Faber and Faber, London, 1946.

Coward, Sir Noel, *The Lyrics of Noel Coward*, Metheun, London, 1983.

Cree, Edward, *The Cree Journals*, Webb & Bower, Exeter, 1981.

Crisswell, Colin N, *The Taipans*, Oxford University Press, 1991.

Dougherty, Paul, *Hong Kong 1968, Hong Kong 1969 and Hong Kong 1970*, Hong Kong Government Information Services.

Dyer Ball, J, *Things Chinese*, John Murray, London, 1904.

Eitel, E J, *Europe in China: The History of Hong Kong*, Kelly & Walsh, Hong Kong, 1895.

Endacott, G B, *A Biographical Sketch-Book of Early Hong Kong*, Eastern Universities Press, Singapore, 1962.

Endacott, G B, *A History of Hong Kong*, Oxford University Press, 1958.

Fox, Grace, *British Admirals and Chinese Pirates 1832-1869*, Kegan Paul, Trench, Trubner & Co, London, 1940.

Grantham, Sir Alexander, *Via Ports*, Hong Kong University Press, 1965.

Hacker, Arthur and Perkins, David, *Hacker's Hong Kong*, Gareth Powell and Ted Thomas, Hong Kong, 1976.

Harfield, Alan, *British and Indian Armies on the China Coast 1785-1985*, A and J Partnership, 1990.

Hayes, J.W. and Smith, Carl T, *Wanchai*, The Journal of the Hong Kong Branch of the Royal Asiatic Society, 1975.

Hoe, Susanna, *The Private Life of Old Hong Kong*, Oxford University Press, Hong Kong, 1991.

Hopkirk, Peter, *The Great Game*, John Murray, 1990.

Hughes, Richard, *Hong Kong: Borrowed Place—Borrowed Time*, Andre Deutsch, 1968.

Hurd, Douglas, *The Arrow War*, Collins, 1967.

Johnston, Reginald, *Twilight in the Forbidden City*, Victor Gollancz Ltd, 1934.

Jung Chang, *Mme Sun Yat-sen*, Penguin Books, London, 1986.

King, Paul, *In the Chinese Customs Service*, Heath Cranton Ltd, London, 1924.

Lane-Poole, Stanley, *Sir Harry Parkes in China*, Methuen & Co, London, 1901.

Lee, James Zee-Ming, *Chinese Potpourri*, Oriental Publishers, Hong Kong, 1950.

Lethbridge, Henry, *Hong Kong: Stability and Change*, Oxford University Press, Hong Kong, 1978.

Lindley, Captain Augustus F., *A Cruise in Chinese Waters*, Cassell, Petter, Galpin & Co., London, 1866.

Lindsay, Oliver, *The Lasting Honour*, Hamish Hamilton Limited, London, 1978.

Luff, John, *Hong Kong Cavalcade*, South China Morning Post, 1868.

Mason, Richard, *The World of Suzie Wong*, William Collins & Co, London, 1957.

Mattock, Kate, *The Story of Government House*, Hong Kong Government Information Services, 1978.

Maunsell Consultants Asia Ltd in association with Urbis Travers Morgan Ltd, *Central and Wanchai Reclamation Development*, Hong Kong Government Territory Development Department, 1993.

McAleavy, Henry, *The Modern History of China*, Weidenfeld and Nicholson, London, 1967.

Norton-Kyshe, James, *The History of the Laws and Courts of Hong Kong*, Vetch and Lee, Hong Kong, 1971.

Oliphant, Laurence, *Narrative of the Earl of Elgin's Mission to China and Japan*, William Blackwood, 1859.

Oxley, Lieutenant Colonel D.H., *Victoria Barracks 1842-1979*, Headquarters British Forces, Hong Kong, 1979.

Papers Relating to Hong Kong, House of Commons, London, 1860.

Peplow, S.H. and Barker, M, *Hongkong, Around and About*, Ye Olde Printerie Ltd, Hong Kong, 1931.

Pinkstone, Mark, *Hong Kong 1982*, Hong Kong Government Information Services, 1982.

Pope-Hennessy, James, *Verandah*, George Allen & Unwin, 1964.

Rodwell, Sally, *Historic Hong Kong*, Odyssey Guides, Hong Kong, 1991.

Sayer, G.R., *Hong Kong 1862-1919*, Hong Kong University Press, 1975.

Smith, Peter, *Victoria's Victories*, Spellmount Ltd, Tunbridge Wells, 1987.

Smith, Carl T, *A Sense of History*, Hong Kong Educational Press, Hong Kong, 1995.

Thomas, David, *Royal Admirals*, Andre Deutsh, London, 1982.

Tobin, Anthony, *Nightlife*, Gulliver Books, Hong Kong, 1979.

Tsai Chin, *Daughter of Shanghai*, Chatto & Windus, London, 1988.

Turner, John, *Kwang Tung or Five Years in China*, S. W. Partridge & Co, 1894.

Waley, Arthur, *The Opium War Through Chinese Eyes*, George Allen and Unwin, London, 1958.

Warner, John, *Hong Kong Illustrated: Views and News 1840-1890*, John Warner Publications, Hong Kong, 1981.

Weithoff, Bodo, *Introduction to Chinese History*, George Allen and Unwin, London, 1971.

Wan Chai District, Wan Chai District Board, Hong Kong, 1992.

PERIODICALS CONSULTED

The China Magazine
The China Mail
The Friend of China
The Hongkong Daily Press
The Hongkong Register
The Hongkong Standard
The Hong Kong Tatler
The Hongkong Telegraph
The Hongkong Weekly Press
The Illustrated London News
The Journal of the Hong Kong Branch, the Royal Asiatic Society
The Morning Herald
The Times
The Wanchai Magazine